Dedication

Agnes Smutny, for her resilience and compassion in the face of trial; Elsie Stafford, for her hearty laugh, kind eyes, and great stories. Kylie and Avery, Kaelyn and Cora, may you have the confidence and strength of your foremothers.

THRIVE

**The Facilitator's Guide to
Radically Inclusive Meetings**

Dr. Mark Smutny

Editors: Gloria Campbell & Barbara Anderson

Published in the United States by

Civic Reinventions. Inc

www.civicreinventions.com

Cover image: © *Vladimir Verano*

Book & cover design:
Vladimir Verano, VertVolta Design
www.vertvoltapress.com

Image rights: Pg 19. © *Can Stock Photo / simo988* ; Pg 20: © *Can Stock Photo / svetap* ; Pg 139: © 2018 *Tim Corey*, www.colibrifacilitation.com. *Used with permission.* Pg 141: © 2019 Jessamy Gee, Think in Colour, *Used with permission.*

ISBN

Print: 978-1-7339281-0-6

ebook: 978-1-7339281-1-3

1. business, 2. meetings; 3. facilitation;
4. how-to; 5. education

Library of Congress Control Number: 2019908438

CONTENTS

Preface

I see a world where everyone is heard, where all people matter. I see communities that embrace all voices and are committed to freedom, justice, and opportunity for all. I see businesses, nonprofits, and the public sector creatively engage people in thousands of ways to get their best ideas, empower the broken, and build a society where all are treated with dignity and respect. I see a people, amazingly diverse, stunningly beautiful, and woven into a tapestry of love, justice, and peace. I see a mosaic of different colors, different hues, different perspectives, different genders; a kaleidoscope of humanity driven by hope, strengthened by courage and the fundamental belief that we are best when we embody the creed of e pluribus unam, "out of many, one."

I wrote *THRIVE: The Facilitator's Guide to Radically Inclusive Meetings* driven by a vision where equality, inclusion, and engagement can happen for every participant in every meeting, conference, and summit. I want your meetings to have energy and imagination and be worth every second of your time. In a word, I want your meetings—all of them—to THRIVE!

I have been facilitating meetings for over a third of a century. I have participated in thousands of meetings. Some sailed along with ease and reached their destination. Some sputtered and stalled. Some never left port. All were attended by people who said they value everyone's participation. But too often, a few people dominated. When the voices of the many were not heard, the meetings were less productive and more frustrating than they could have been.

Diverse voices and inclusive meeting designs help organizations thrive. A mix of perspectives, life experience, and other forms of diversity reveal greater truth than any one of them alone. When groups are mostly of one gender, or one race and ethnicity, much is lost. The group is less imaginative. When people of different genders, races, and ethnicities meet, groups think better, see better, and are better.

I believe equality and equity are more than lofty words. They are practices. We practice equality by being even-handed, impartial and fair. We embody equity by the way we respect and include every voice and each perspective. Embodying these values throughout our meetings and organizations makes space for us to rise to what President Lincoln called "the better angels of our nature." We become more open, curious, and respectful. Justice for all becomes more than a slogan. It becomes a way of life. The result is better outcomes, more productivity, and more motivated employees, volunteers, and stakeholders.

Think of meetings in which a few people dominated. Remember how most people stayed quiet, doodled, or texted until a break in the meeting. Then recall the noise level during breaks as conversation erupted. The purpose of this book is to help you bring the energy of break time into your meetings. I will teach you how, with good meeting design and a few techniques and tools, to include those voices and energy in your meetings, no matter the size or occasion.

Whether you are a facilitator, a nonprofit or business leader, a public official or consultant, this book is written for you. Community organizers, planners, board and committee members, religious leaders and adherents—no matter the size of your group or meeting--will find help in this book.

This book covers multiple topics to help your meetings thrive. I begin with a chapter on disastrous meetings. We all have a list of similar experiences. These painful memories inspire my passion and vision for better meetings that embrace every voice.

I follow with a chapter on the core values of radical equality, equity, and inclusion. These values are the heartbeat of everything else I say. Next, I examine the nature of conversational leadership and its implications for our meetings and organizations.

With a foundation in the values of inclusivity and an organization-wide commitment to nurturing strategic conversations, I provide wisdom to ready yourself to lead and facilitate meetings. Preparation begins with developing emotional resilience, achieving mindfulness, and becoming a proficient listener.

In the chapter, *Structuring an Agenda*, I give an outline of the elements needed in every well-run, inclusive meeting. These include:

- Listening
- Drafting an agenda
- Welcome
- Introductions
- Becoming fully present
- Ground rules
- Review of the agenda
- Issues, questions, and process
- Clarifying outcomes and summarizing next steps
- Evaluation

This chapter is the go-to-chapter when you need a quick summary of what to include in meetings you facilitate.

Then I go deeper into each aspect. I describe meeting elements that launch a good meeting including centering, icebreakers, and ground rules.

The chapter, *Flexible Roles in Groups*, gives tips for how to be an effective facilitator in any group. It is a great, accessible training resource for people new to facilitation.

In the following chapters, I introduce a variety of meeting designs that engender inclusivity and full participation. These include framing questions that invite energy and imagination, simple meeting designs that engage all voices in a short time, and a variety of whole group planning methods that have emerged in the past three decades. All are rooted in the values of inclusion and what I call "radical equality." These methods include Appreciative Inquiry, World Café, Open Space, and other formats. All combine small group conversations with larger plenary sessions.

I dedicate a chapter to techniques and tools that help diverse groups thrive, followed by a chapter on multilingual gatherings. I help you discover practices that embrace voices and perspectives cross-culturally. I also write about including persons with disabilities in your meetings and outline meeting accommodations.

The next chapters help facilitators in special circumstances. Chapters on negotiation techniques and facilitating conflict will teach you how to navigate treacherous water. These chapters are particularly useful in these polarized times.

A chapter on strategic plans summarizes how to make a strategic planning process inclusive of all stakeholders in an organization. It gives practical ways for your strategic plan to avoid the destiny of many others—being ignored as they gather dust on a shelf.

If you want to make a system-wide change in your organization, read the chapter on organizational change. The insights apply to all kinds of change initiatives from implementing values of diversity, equity, and inclusion; to technological change, embracing new markets, and breaking down organizational silos.

The next chapter is a how-to on helping groups of all types become mindful of patterns in their history that shape the way they behave today and respond to the future. Awareness of these patterns makes groups more likely to move forward with health, optimism, and renewed energy.

The concluding chapters explore ways to record, conclude, and evaluate meetings. I toss in a chapter on writing well. As facilitators and leaders, we write emails, memos, and reports every day. Writing that is simple, clean, and devoid of extra verbiage and clutter strengthens our work and the groups we serve. I provide a checklist for assembling a meetings toolkit beyond markers and tape.

Then I discuss the circumstances when it is best to hire a professional facilitator. While I hope this book helps you become a skilled facilitator, circumstances do arise when your group needs an outside facilitator and consultant. I briefly discuss when and how a professional facilitator can help your group, conference, or summit.

I conclude with suggestions for further reading to expand your facilitation repertoire.

I want your meetings to thrive. I want them to reach their destination without capsizing. I want them to produce positive results, not frustration and boredom. My deepest wish is that you will never attend another pointless meeting where the few pontificate and the many stay quiet. My hope and prayer are that your meetings will be a beautiful tapestry of unity, difference, and inclusion. I hope that, with insights from this book, all your meetings will thrive, and you will sail along to your heart's content.

Acknowledgments

I cannot express the depth of my gratitude to Barbara Anderson, my wife and colleague. Barbara taught me three-quarters of what I know about meeting facilitation, beginning in graduate school. Whether she was in meetings with Harvard professors, graduate students, neighborhood people, or church folk, she made meetings thrive. I saw how her empathic spirit helped groups grow closer. I saw how a light but firm touch enabled groups to function better. I saw how her commitment to equity and inclusion sought out the contributions of everyone. I discovered how a skilled facilitator could change the dynamics of a meeting from frustration to productive and fun. Barbara models an optimistic spirit and an open heart. Her writing style is journalistic, simple, and clean. She's been cleaning up my bloated writing for years. Thank you, love of my life. You're the best.

Many others deserve my thanks. Larry Hill, campus minister at Boston-Cambridge Ministry in Higher Education at Harvard-Radcliffe, taught me the principles and practices of community organizing in the mode of Saul Alinsky. Harvey Cox introduced me to the teachings of Paulo Freire and Ernesto Cardenal. Dieter Georgi was a spell-binding storyteller as was my maternal grandmother, Elsie Stafford. William C. Schram ran tight meetings with authority. Eric Law opened up a world of inclusive meeting practices.

I am grateful for the hundreds of meetings in which energy surged, and each participant felt his or her contribution mattered. From great facilitators, I learned what makes meetings thrive.

I am even grateful for the hundreds of meetings I have endured (and sometimes led) in which the topics were pointless, the facilitator clueless, and I practiced doodling—an obsessive-compulsive habit of mine. I learned much about what not to do as a facilitator and that I will never be an artist.

I thank the groups and organizations that invited me to consult with them or elected me to serve as their chair and chief facilitator: business groups, residents' associations, training institutes, homeless shelters, affordable housing agencies, regional planning commissions, mayoral transition teams, public/private partnerships, public policy advocacy groups, transportation coalitions, all types of governmental advisory groups, good government working groups, multicultural training institutes, and churches galore.

I am grateful for my two editors, Barbara Anderson and Gloria Campbell, who made my manuscript clean and simple. Ernie Cathcart, Staci Haber, Kristina Mayer, Thomas Gold, and Aaron Morrow read the manuscript and gave dozens of helpful suggestions. I thank Vladimir Verano who prepared the manuscript for publication and designed the cover.

I am immensely grateful for the privileges I have been given: great parents, a wonderful family, sons and daughters-in-law, and four delightful granddaughters: Kylie, Avery, Kaelyn, and Cora. I'm grateful for the best education imaginable and for the gift of life itself.

As a white male, married, heterosexual professional with all the privileges granted therein, I am mindful that many in our beautiful and fragile world are oppressed, abused, and forgotten. Maybe, in some small way, this book will help those who have been historically excluded to find their voice. The beating heart of this book is a commitment to embrace inclusion and equity in our meeting and to honor and engage every voice. Thanks to all who made THRIVE possible! I am eternally grateful.

The Author

Dr. Mark Smutny is a professional facilitator, consultant, speaker, author, and Founder of Civic Reinventions, Inc. He is known for helping organizations uncover the wisdom hidden in their diversity, build cohesion, and achieve their goals.

He draws upon decades of work planning and leading retreats, facilitating meetings, and working with nonprofits and businesses. He teaches and writes on the arts of effective facilitation. He has worked in the fields of homeless services, affordable housing, transportation services for special needs populations, business and resident associations, faith-based groups, and public/private partnerships dedicated to strengthening civic engagement.

Mark received his Master of Divinity degree from the Harvard Divinity School, one of the most religiously diverse theological institutions in the world. His doctorate focused on organizational revitalization in multicultural settings. He is a Program Associate with the Kaleidoscope Institute, an agency that equips leaders to communicate effectively across cultures, ethnicities, and race.

When not working, Mark and his wife, Barbara Anderson, enjoy the Cascades, cooking, gardening, exercising their dogs, and playing with their granddaughters.

You can learn more about Mark Smutny and Civic Reinventions, Inc. professional facilitation services, consulting, coaching, and training at www.civicreinventions.com or by calling 626-676-0287.

THRIVE

Introduction

When did you facilitate your first meeting? My first meeting was in the fourth grade. I had been elected captain of my fourth-grade basketball team at Bickel Elementary School in Twin Falls, Idaho, my hometown. The captain had the privilege of naming the team. I named them the Smutny Sharpshooters. We were diverse: Santos Salinas, Jesse Hernandez, Ricardo Montez, and David Galvin joined Michael Fuller, Michael Covington, Gary Cooper, and me. The boys with Spanish names had parents born in Mexico. I was half Czech. The others sounded like their families arrived on the Mayflower. We had no coach, only yours truly.

The first meeting was during lunch hour on the asphalt playground. It wasn't much of a basketball court. The stripes marking the court boundaries were faded. The hoops had no net. Bickel was the poor elementary school in town. A third of the student body came from South Park where redlining forced Mexican Americans to live. The remainder were farm kids. I was reared on a dairy farm. Hard work, sports, church, and family defined my upbringing.

At the first meeting of the Smutny Sharpshooters, I knew enough about coaching to know it was not a democracy. However, if I simply ordered people around there would be a revolt. I knew I needed to keep it short and clear, have my teammates practice a few exercises, and mostly let them play basketball.

The biggest challenge was the boy who was unable to reach the hoop with his shot. In the language of the time, he was uncoordinated. I taught him to engage his entire body when shooting hoops. By getting him to push up with his legs, torso, and arms like unleashing a coiled spring, he was able to shoot the ball to the elusive goal. He beamed when he made his first shot. The rest of the team cheered. I was hooked on coaching—a form of facilitation.

I learned through that experience that one job of a facilitator is to cheer. Encouragement is central if you want a group to thrive, whether a sports team or a board of directors. Basic skills are equally important.

Reaching the goal, building community, and including everyone helps the group thrive. With these basic skills, you've got a team, and you're on your way to a good meeting.

We went on to lose most of our games. The teams from the richer side of town had adult coaches who knew what they were doing. I'll never forget when, in the heat of a game, David Galvin made a shot from twenty-five feet—amazing for a fourth grader. I'll also never forget my first homemade, freshly-baked tortilla that Ricardo Montez's mother made one afternoon after basketball practice. I had been invited to Ricardo's home as our little team bonded. The steaming tortilla, slathered with butter and cinnamon sugar, was unbelievably tasty.

I learned a lot about facilitation in fourth grade: exude calm authority, encourage the team, and let others shine. Teach basic skills and practice them. Have fun. Don't be too serious. Work toward a common goal. Cheer a lot. Eat afterward.

Since those days on the playground, I have participated in thousands of meetings. In graduate school I helped plan and organize a peace conference at the Kennedy School of Government during the height of the arms race—we met twenty times to pull off the event. We attracted twelve hundred people from all over Massachusetts. As a Presbyterian pastor in Ohio, New York, California, and Washington State, I participated in as many meetings as stars in the sky. Some were poorly run and I was able to catch up on missed sleep. I've also experienced meetings run so well that I never wanted them to end.

I have chaired hundreds of meetings: for local and regional governments, private/public partnerships, business groups, and non-profits. I've led hundreds of strategy meetings. I've helped plan everything from how best to win a mayoral election to what size placemats should decorate dining tables. I've coached soccer, organized food drives, and held meetings with traumatized victims of police sweeps clearing homeless camps under freeways. I've served on boards of directors, consulted with governments, and revitalized citizen groups. I have earned my reputation as a professional facilitator.

Meetings are a fact of life. At work and play; in all walks of life; in all disciplines; in the public, private, and nonprofit sectors we meet. We meet incessantly for good and for ill.

All of us have stories about poor meetings. Some of us have stories of great meetings. The difference between poor and great meetings often depends on the skill of the facilitator, how the meeting is structured, and whether diversity is embraced. The root of the word facilitation means "to make easy." I want to make easy all the meetings you attend or facilitate.

Fortunately, facilitation can be learned. Various arts of facilitation organize the chapters of this book. I encourage you to read the book cover-to-cover and then pick and choose ideas as they best fit your context. I hope you discover the joy of a well-run meeting. May you and your organization thrive, and may all your meetings be easy. As Captain Picard ordered in every episode of Star Trek: The Next Generation, "Make it so."

Disastrous Meetings

Before we enter deep space and a journey to great meetings, memories of meeting disasters rear their ugly heads. From painful schoolyard confabs gossiping about who should receive valentines and who should not, from parliamentary assemblies so confused by amendments to amendments to amendments that a bucket of Drano couldn't get the meeting unstuck, to conferences so tedious we caught up on the year's sleep deficit, we all recall meeting disasters. I will list a few.

- Meetings where there is no apparent agenda and the facilitator sits clueless about how to move the meeting along.

- Meetings where expectations are perfectly unclear.

- Meetings so stultifyingly boring that fantasies of being fired illicit orgasms of joy.

- Meetings where a handful dominate while dozens remain silent.

- Meetings dominated by men with few women present.

- Meetings absent of diversity and marked by groupthink.

- Meetings attended by people from a variety of cultures but dominated by the majority culture, usually white.

- Meetings where experts drone on about technical topics illustrated by PowerPoint slides that no one can see.

- Meetings where senior officials mandate new policies and line employees who know the policies will not work are never asked their opinions.

- Meetings where half the participants are checking their smartphones, writing emails, and wondering what to cook for dinner. The other half dreams of Hawaii.

- Meetings where the next steps are ignored. The same meeting with the same ideas is repeated annually.

- Meetings constrained with limits on how long an individual can speak, resulting in anger, frustration, and being cut-off.

- Meetings so polarized and divided that people vow never to attend another meeting again.

My wife says the list is long enough, so I'll stop. It illustrates the day-to-day experience most of us have. Lousy meetings waste our time, frustrate our dreams, and force us to consider becoming a hermit. Meetings dominated by a few lack energy and imagination.

However, it need not be. I have experienced hundreds of meetings where the excitement is palpable, the energy pulsating, and the results tangible and clear. I have facilitated meetings where participants are fully present and engaged. Meetings that look like a mosaic of humanity make for vibrant, creative results.

As a professional facilitator and consultant, I know that listening is central to the success of organizations I seek to help. So, listen. Listen carefully to the heartbeat of your group or organization. I dream that by using the tools in this book and listening, you and the people you meet with will thrive.

Cultural Mindfulness
and Radical Inclusion

The central values informing this book are equality, inclusion, and diversity. These are both principles and practices. As a principle, inclusion is a goal that helps organizations envision a world in which all are heard, and no one is left out. As a practice, inclusion uses practical tools to help organizations embody fairness.

The inclusion of diverse perspectives increases productivity. When groups embrace multiple perspectives and life experiences, the result is better thinking and more creativity, as demonstrated by multiple studies. Organizations suffer when they waste the gifts of introverts, women, and culturally-less-dominant persons. This chapter focuses on cultural mindfulness and a commitment to radical inclusion. The chapter, *Facilitating Culturally Diverse Meetings,* describes meeting techniques and tools that embody inclusion.

The journey toward greater inclusion begins with developing an awareness of the power of unconscious cultural assumptions. Assumptions about power—who has it and who does not—can inhibit fairness. Hidden attitudes about leadership, hierarchy, and communication styles contribute to verbosity in some and silence in others.

These assumptions are at play when men are treated more favorably than women, Caucasians given more respect than people of color, and the affluent invited to speak more than poor people. Exclusive attitudes, often unconscious, are evident when immigrants are less regarded than long-time citizens; persons with disabilities have diminished roles in groups; openly LGBTQ people are relegated to the sidelines. Cultural mindfulness of these assumptions is the beginning of a journey toward more productive groups.

I believe in the radical equality of all human beings. No human is of greater or lesser value than anyone else. The word "radical" has in its beginnings the word "root," meaning what is foundational. I believe the commitment to radical equality is the root, or foundation, of inclusive meeting practices and fair facilitation.

When we embody radical equality as the foundation of our meetings, meetings function better. No one resents being left out. When we are mindful of privilege and facilitate fairly, the values of equality, equity, and fairness become real. We embody what we most care about.

My journey toward cultural mindfulness, always a work in progress, includes decades of reflection. Permit me an extended narrative. Your story will be different.

I grew up with family stories of compassion and social justice. During the Great Depression, my maternal grandparents provided hospitality to lost and hungry men. Whenever Grandpa Stafford was in town, he struck up conversations with unemployed men down on their luck and brought them back to the farm in his Model A pickup truck. My grandmother fixed a hearty meal, fed the men in her farmhouse kitchen, and gave them a warm place to spend the night. Bellies were filled, stories shared, and laughter, too. Compassion and an open heart were central to my grandparents' way of life.

When President Franklin Roosevelt's Executive Order 9066 in 1942 incarcerated thousands of Japanese Americans in concentration camps in America's interior, my grandparents fought back. They successfully petitioned local authorities to allow two Japanese American farm families to live on the Stafford property. Conservatives in a conservative community, they believed fiercely in equality.

My parents taught me that Mexican immigrant laborers who plant, weed, and harvest American's fruits and vegetables, milk America's cows, and staff America's butcher houses, deserve respect. I still remember going with my parents when I was a child to the Twin Falls, Idaho, Labor Camp to deliver food and clothes. I was horrified by the dirt floors, winter drafts, and open sewers that conflicted with everything my parents believed. That was the first time I saw something so compromising of human dignity.

My family of origin ran a small business: a dairy farm. Work was constant. I learned compassion from both parents and how to treat animals with firmness, not harshness. I observed how well the division of labor between my mom and dad worked. Dad was outside milking cows, cultivating fields, and harvesting crops. Mom ran the office—accounting, payroll, and all kinds of reports. It was a co-equal relationship. Mom could also drive the big trucks and do whatever was needed. On the other hand, Dad never did learn to cook. He perfected cooking ignorance in the kitchen.

Despite the equal importance of their roles, I saw numerous employees dismiss my mother's intelligence and authority because of her gender. My mother hates being discounted. Those employees were mistaken to underestimate her. I learned to share her anger and to respect women fully. Equality of gender is not merely a concept. It is a daily practice that respects the voices of both women and men.

For me, the journey toward greater mindfulness and the radical equality of all people came with fits and starts. The moral arc of the universe may bend toward justice, but I go two steps forward and one step back.

In college, a dear friend confronted me about my homophobic words. I changed. When I headed off to Harvard University for a master's degree in social ethics, my cultural awareness grew further. Harvard Divinity School's diversity was impressive. Christians of all types (Protestant, Catholic, and Orthodox), Conservative and Reformed Jews, Shiite and Sunni Muslims, Buddhists, Sikhs, Hindus, Zoroastrians, and Humanists studied and ate and attended classes together. We listened to one another and grew in respect for each other. Our inter-religious, racially diverse global community was united in academic rigor and mutual respect. For a farm kid from Idaho who had never been east of the Mississippi River, this was an eye-opening, heavenly experience.

In the words of the as-seen-on-T.V. hawker, "Wait. There's more." My first roommate at Harvard Divinity School was named Alton Pollard, III. I imagined that he was going to be a white, Ivy League prep school graduate with that fancy name and I dreaded meeting him. But when Alton Pollard walked into our shared domicile, he blew away my stereotype. Alton was an African American man from suburban Minneapolis. He had also assumed he was being paired with a white man of financial privilege and was pleased to find a farm boy from Idaho instead.

Two people could not be more different. In a dorm room on the third floor of Divinity Hall, we talked for hours that night. Alton told me his story of heartache and rage when his white friends abandoned him during a high school race riot. In the aftermath, he vowed to attend the all-black Fisk University where he wouldn't have to deal with clueless white classmates. I grew up on a dairy farm in one of the whitest states in America. Stories cascaded. Stories of hate and fear and finding safety from racism's cruelty. Stories about family, friends, hopes, and dreams. By providence, we were roommates.

Two weeks later, Alton invited me to attend the historical, African American, Second Baptist Church of Roxbury. Its pastor, a burly giant of a man, welcomed me with a resonant voice and a handshake that swallowed my hand. He told me I would read the scripture in worship that morning because I was a seminary student. I did not tell him I had never helped lead worship in any stripe of church—black, white, or brown.

When the time came, I climbed up to the pulpit, opened the large Bible and looked out on a sea of faces. Ladies in beautiful hats and men in three-piece suits waited to hear a word of hope. I was the lone white face amid hundreds of souls. My heart pounded, and my voice quivered. Here is what I read from the prophet Isaiah:

> *God gives power to the faint and strengthens the powerless. Even youths will faint and be weary, and the young will fall exhausted; but those who wait for the Lord shall renew their strength, they shall mount up with wings like eagles, they shall run and not be weary, they shall walk and not faint (Isaiah 40:29-31).*

After worship, two petite women in their eighties wearing gorgeous hats spoke words I have never forgotten, "Your being here gives us hope." I was stunned. I hadn't done anything. I had merely shown up with my pale, freckled skin and carrot-top hair and read scripture in public for the first time in my life. However, these two dear angels spoke of hope.

Later that day, I learned the context of their words. Only a year before, Boston had erupted in race riots. White "Southies" from South Boston pitted themselves against African Americans. The iconic *Boston Globe* photo of a white Bostonian using an American flag to threaten a black Bostonian still lingered in people's memories like a knife cutting into raw flesh.

For all they knew, those sweet women may have thought I was an Irish American Catholic from South Boston instead of a half Czech, Presbyterian farm kid from Idaho. "Your being here gives us hope." Maybe they saw me as one of the few with my complexion who had the guts to show up in their church, the center of their community life. In their lifelong experience of racism, they caught a glimmer of hope in this redheaded seminarian. "Those who wait for the Lord shall renew their strength, they shall mount up with wings like eagles, they shall run and not be weary, they shall walk and not faint."

I vowed that day to do what I could with my life to bring about racial reconciliation. If these two women who had been through a lifetime of hate and fear thought I gave them hope, then I should probably take their words seriously. I will never know the fullness of their pain. My position of privilege shields me from the worst. My compassion and empathy only go so far.

Still, when those dear women spoke of hope, they sparked a flame of hope inside me. Hope. Hope is what we do each day when we take one step toward inclusion and justice. Hope is action. Action toward a world that is more just, more compassionate, and more beautiful. We act our way into hope.

The words of those African American women are seared in my memory as if by purifying fire. Ever since, I have felt called to build inclusive, equitable communities and organizations. I trace a direct line from the words of those two classy ladies to the calling of my life.

But wait. There's more. In those heady graduate school days, Harvard Divinity School recruited feminist scholars from around the world and liberation theologians from Latin America, African American communities and Asia. Ethicists from around the world opened the doors of my mind to perspectives I had never encountered.

That is where I fell in love with a feminist theology student who became my colleague and wife. The Reverend Dr. Barbara Anderson and I have sought to embed equality in all dimensions of our lives. We shared jobs equally and served together as co-pastors for decades. We shared domestic and parenting duties. I cooked, and Barbara helped. We spent equal time at home caring for our children. She carried our two babies in her womb and breastfed. When our boys woke up in the middle of the night hungry, I fetched them. I raised vegetables and mowed the lawn. She did finances. I put chains on our tires in blizzards, and she kept the car warm.

All these stories convey a lifelong commitment to inclusion. Nevertheless, for years I had limited awareness of my cultural privilege. As it turns out, I score high in privilege in nearly every category.

I am a white, American, heterosexual, highly-educated professional. I am tall with a deep, resonant, baritone voice. I am married, and my parents are still married after more than 60 years. My upbringing was privileged relative to most of the world. We never lacked food or shelter. In graduate school, I studied with the best from all over the world. I am at ease around politicians and corporate executives, professors, farm workers, and day laborers. I own my house and two cars and have never gone without food except when ill. I have been unemployed for no more than three weeks of my entire life. By every measure, I am privileged.

Being mindful of these privileges is a start. Being mindful of the ignorance privilege can bestow launches the journey toward inclusion. For example, I do not know what it is like to be an African American male walking down any street in America or what it is like to carry a baby inside me, as many women do. I will never be a poor Guatemalan immigrant mother seeking refuge in America for her children. But I do know that I don't know how those experiences feel. I can try to imagine their fear, strength, and courage, but it is not like living it.

Privilege tends to create cultural blindness. Many whites are defensive and angry at charges of racism, sexism, or homophobia. For example, I hear white colleagues insist angrily that America's election of Barak Obama as President proves the United States is now color-blind and that racism is no more. I've heard whites declare there are no jobs for white males anymore because brown-skinned immigrants have snatched them. I've also heard that women are completely equal to men in the workplace. However, none of these statements is true.

Systemic racism and sexism remain pervasive, even as the U.S. has made much progress. As recently as 2018, several state legislatures enacted policies that disenfranchise poor people, people whose jobs have inflexible hours, Blacks, and Latinos. Local governments still invest in infrastructure where the affluent and middle-class live while neglecting new immigrant neighborhoods and those with a high percentage of people of color. Unemployment for young, African Americans males numbers in the 30% range compared to 4% for white males. As of this writing, only 5% of Fortune 500 CEOs are women.

My unofficial survey of meetings shows that white males do most of the speaking, both in the percentage of people and length of time. Also, ideas put forth by women and people of color are later frequently attributed to the white men present. In self-confession, I am still guilty of this more often than I realize. The antidote is for white men and people of privilege to self-monitor and to be held accountable. Old habits die hard. Hands loosen their grip on power only when someone else helps pry them loose. Replacing white fear and male fear with humility, awareness, and empathy is a long journey home to the promise of America—equality and justice for all.

How do we put a commitment to radical equality and equity into action? Embodying inclusion begins with cultural self-awareness. Culture is far more than the food we eat, the songs we listen to, and how we dress. A person's cultural makeup includes race, ethnicity, skin color, gender, sexual orientation, education, marital status, age, physical ability, and medical status. It includes religion, economic status, profession, nationality, military background, geographical location, language, attitudes about leadership and followership, myths that shape behavior, and assumptions about how we communicate with one another.

Becoming mindful of these cultural attributes is a lifelong discipline. For the privileged, it sometimes takes a metaphorical club on the head to begin the journey. More often than not, cultural awareness begins with being quiet and listening. Regular exposure to people different from you helps if coupled with a willing spirit and an open mind. Training in cultural competency helps build mindfulness. Self-awareness and a humble spirit help as well.

Cultural mindfulness for people of privilege is like helping a fish understand that it is swimming in water. Cultural mindfulness is easier for those who experience discrimination daily. When bigotry and hate assault a person every day in large and small ways, awareness of one's difference is constant.

One of my mentors, Eric Law, recommends developing awareness of one's privilege and culture by convening a small group to share lists of cultural attributes. Each person writes down his or her cultural attributes and is invited to share the results. After each person has an opportunity to share, the group discusses what they notice and what they wonder about. Here are three examples of completed Cultural Attribute Inventories.

Mark Smutny

Race – Caucasian

Ethnicity – White

Skin color – Pale with freckles

Hair color – Red, fading to white

Gender – Male

Sexual orientation – Straight

Education – Bachelor's and Master's degrees, Doctorate

Marital status – Married

Age – Young older adult – 63 years old

Physical ability – Able-bodied

Medical status – Healthy

Religion – Liberal Protestant Christian

Economic status – Middle Class

Profession – Professional facilitator, consultant, writer, clergyman, small business owner, manager

Employment History – Farm worker, janitor, handyman, conference organizer, community organizer, speaker, senior pastor, facilities manager, manager of a homeless shelter, transportation manager, entrepreneur, professional facilitator, consultant, writer, and speaker.

Nationality – American

Military background – None

Geographical location – Urban/suburban northwestern U.S.

Language – English

In the hierarchy of privilege, I score somewhere between the stratosphere and outer space.

A Colleague

Race – Black

Ethnicity – African American

Skin color – Light brown

Hair color – Black

Gender – Male

Sexual orientation – Straight

Education – Bachelor's and Master's degrees

Marital status – Married

Age – Forties

Physical ability – Able-bodied

Medical status – Healthy

Religion – None

Economic status – Middle class

Profession – Social worker, human services director, nonprofit director

Employment history – Caseworker, homeless services manager, director of transportation services

Nationality – American

Military background – None

Geographical location – Urban and suburban American northwest

Language – English

He scores high and low. He is at neither the top or bottom of the cultural hierarchy.

A Friend

Race – Mixed race

Ethnicity – Latina

Skin color – Olive

Hair color – Black

Gender – Female

Sexual orientation – Straight

Education – High School

Marital status – Single

Age – Thirties

Physical ability – Able-bodied

Medical status – Healthy

Religion – Roman Catholic

Economic status – Middle Class

Profession – Small Business Owner

Employment history – Army sergeant, sales intern, sales associate, web designer, small business owner

Nationality – American

Military background – Four years in Army

Geographical location – Urban Los Angeles

Language – English, Spanish

Again, she is a mix of high and low privilege.

When I first completed this cultural awareness exercise twenty years ago, I was hit between the eyes by how privileged I am. It changed the way I see my place in the world and its people. I can no longer ignore the power of my privilege and the cultural attitudes I carry with me every day.

When unrecognized, cultural assumptions lead to exclusive behaviors. The more privileged dominate while the less privileged stay quiet, withdraw, or rebel. Unhealthy dynamics born of unconscious cultural assumptions breed inequality and exclusion. When we become culturally mindful, we take a positive first step toward inclusion.

Strengthening cultural awareness is a lifelong task. Many techniques and processes have been invented to assist this effort. One common technique for groups is to explore cultural awareness through the Iceberg Metaphor for Culture first developed by Edward T. Hall. This exercise stimulates reflection on the unconscious cultural attitudes that, like an iceberg, lie below the surface. Cultural attributes above the surface are the ones we commonly recall: food, dress, music—all behaviors we can see, feel, hear, and observe. Those underwater include beliefs, operating myths, values, and notions about leadership and fairness.

Listing all the items above the water is easy. For example, I like burgers and sushi. My musical preferences include folk rock from the sixties and early seventies, Willie Nelson, and Beethoven's Ninth Symphony. I celebrate Easter as the most important holiday of the year. I have six sport coats and a pair of cowboy boots. Bridge is my favorite card game. I like Texas barbeque, Kentucky bourbon, and corn on the cob. Once a year, I smoke a cigar. I like to fly-fish.

Becoming mindful of unconscious attitudes and behaviors below the surface poses a greater challenge. I am driven—working hard was drilled into me as a child growing up on a dairy farm where work is constant, dirty, and demanding. Farm families work all day, from before sunup to after sundown. It is hard for me to slow down. I believe being on time is a virtue. I consider being late to be a sign of an undisciplined mind, although I suspect I am a bit anal retentive when it comes to time.

I find solace in the outdoors and nature's beauty. Working in the fields provides lots of quiet and solitude. Because of that experience, I need some quiet, introverted time every day. Constant chatter drives me crazy. I am passionate about social justice. Cruelty in people and politicians is a cardinal sin. Compassion is the greatest gift. Faith is not a set of beliefs but a set of practices: loving one another and bringing hope to a broken world. I expect to be heard, always. I find it hard to suppress my opinions. I believe the causes of poverty are complex and that most of us affluent, privileged people are clueless about the agony many people in our world face on a day-to-day basis.

Your list will be different. You may be vegan and prefer handmade pasta. You may have deep-seated fears rooted in a history of abuse. Oppression's load may scar you and make you suspicious of all privilege. You may believe that play, not hard work, is a worthy goal. You may believe all religions are delusions. You may make decisions by carefully weighing all options, or you may decide by gut and intuition.

Generate a list of observable cultural attributes above the water and the more subtle values, attitudes, and assumptions that lie hidden beneath the surface. Find a partner and share your discoveries.

Become culturally mindful for yourself and bring that awareness to the groups you facilitate. Even better, carry it into all parts of your life. Let it change the way you view the world and your place in it.

The Art of Conversational Leadership

Advanced warning: This chapter is slightly theoretical. I want you, the reader, to see the role conversation plays in vital organizations and to encourage you as a facilitator to embody practices that maximize inclusive, all-hands-on-deck conversations. When organizations capitalize on the role conversation plays in human interaction, the result is greater creativity and ability to respond to change.

I lead a nonprofit transportation program of sixty-five people that provides free rides for seniors and persons with disabilities. Our shuttle van drivers provide a lifeline to people who otherwise would be isolated and unable to get to the market, doctor, cultural events, or recreation. The program has been around for more than two decades and does important work. It is part of a larger nonprofit providing programs for older adults. It is a great organization.

When I began my job, I listened a lot. I met with all types of employees: drivers, dispatchers, reservationists, managers, and the top levels of administration. I tried to absorb as much as possible of the organization's narrative and practices.

I listened to stories of my predecessor through the lens of the office staff that I manage and my superiors. I wanted to get a collective picture of her leadership style, personality, and the ways she communicated. I knew she had a large imprint on my program. To be effective, I needed to understand everything I could about her and the ways she had shaped the agency. These conversations were essential for how I developed my role and leadership style in this position.

A recurring theme emerged of an organization hungry for senior managers to listen and care. As one of my mentors once said, "Half of leadership is showing up." I learned that while some senior managers understood the importance of listening to line employees and regularly stopped by our site to chat, others did not. Some seemed to know that lower level employees had wisdom for the organization. Others followed an organizational model in which those with authority issue orders and slaves carry out Pharaoh's directives. The problem with this Pharaoh/slave model is that successful, complex organizations do not operate that way.

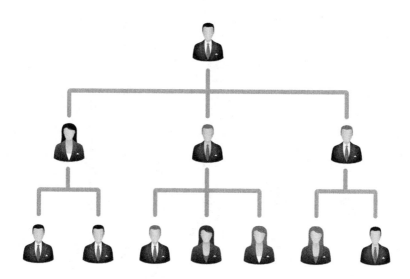

Here is a typical organizational chart in which the mental model resembles ancient Egypt's Pharaonic dictatorship.

The shape of a top-down, Pharaoh-at-the-top, organizational model is a pyramid. No wonder the ancient Israelites revolted and headed to the Promised Land. They did all the work, got none of the credit, liked the idea of freedom to set their own rules, and headed out of town.

Typically used to depict lines of authority, with a few people at the top and many at the bottom, the model is deficient in several ways. Most importantly, neither the pyramid nor the hierarchical organizational chart conveys how relationships and conversations in organizations work.

An organizational chart like the above is a dated mental model. Here is a more dynamic and accurate dynamic.

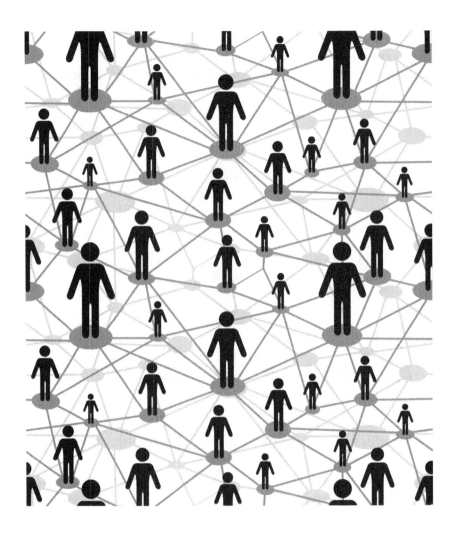

This diagram represents a maze of interacting conversations with lines of connection going to and fro and back and forth. It shows organizations as a web of interacting relationships instead of a pyramid from ancient Egypt.

The diagram illustrates how conversations work in complex organizations. Conversations link lower level employees with one another and those who have more organizational authority. Line employees imagine how to strengthen services, raise capital or improve marketing for products and services. They talk with one another and refine their ideas. If upper leadership listens, the idea generated on "the bottom" shapes and improves the direction of the entire organization.

The art of conversational leadership is to recognize, nurture, and harness these interactive lines of communication in an organization-wide engagement process. All the facilitation techniques in this book encourage multi-layered, interwoven networks of conversation. Instead of only a few at the top talking, the conversations of everyone are encouraged, facilitated, and captured. Now I confess, being on the top of the food chain has its perks. In my career, I have enjoyed being top dog more than once. I also confess that for years I acted out of a mental model that was pharaonic. I assumed that being at the top of the hierarchy meant that I knew more than everyone else. Humility came knocking on my door. I realize now that line workers know far more than I know about direct service delivery. I especially listen to those who get paid little. They tend to know far more about resilience and courage than I. Seeing wisdom in all people, regardless of social location, is a far better way to work, live and view the world. I encourage you to see this way as well.

Here is an example of how an organization's success is limited or expanded by the mental model of its leadership. A few years ago, I worked with a nonprofit that served the homeless and under-housed. They ran several shelters for men, women, and families, and developed and managed affordable housing projects. I was the start-up manager for one of their shelters, a pilot program that received homeless persons caught up in police sweeps. Our goal was to place these traumatized survivors into permanent housing as soon as possible. It was demanding and rewarding work. I supervised counselors, case managers, and house staff. I made sure our neighbors stayed happy and our landowner, a church, as well.

The organization's fund development department had a big job: raise funds, write grants, organize an annual gala, meet application deadlines, and keep donors happy and thanked. They were generating funds for a great organization and could have used all the help they could get. They were hindered by the pyramid-shaped mental model under which the organization operated. In this framework, only the development department, CEO, and Board of Directors could raise the hundreds of thousands of needed dollars. The leaders thought that neither site managers nor line employees would have the experience, knowledge, or contacts to raise funds for what the community knew were essential services.

However, nearly every employee did have fundraising experience. Some had worked on church-based stewardship campaigns, others had volunteered at a phone bank, and still others had organized fundraising events for schools. All of them had a web of relationships, friends, family, and neighbors who, if asked, would have given to the good work of sheltering and housing people down on their luck.

However, with a hierarchical mental model for the organization, they were never asked. If they had been, their ideas might have raised funds from sources that had never given before, averted a severe budget crisis, and revitalized the organization.

Imagine if each employee (there were eighteen in my shelter) had been invited to list ten persons they knew well who could be approached to give $25 - $100 or more for the work of their particular shelter. In our case, 18 employees x 10 contacts x $50 = $9,000. That's a chunk of change towards a social worker's salary.

If line employees had been asked for ideas, maybe they would have organized a phone-a-thon or hosted a community meal at the shelter and invited people with means to give. Maybe one or two would have invited ten people into their homes to hear stories from people who made it successfully out of shelter into housing. Good food could be served and libations, too. Then they would serve up a request and ask the attendees to pull out their checkbooks.

This fundraising example demonstrates why the mental model of a web is superior to that of a pyramid. Leaders who understand that all organizations are a complex web of relationships instead of a hierarchical flow-chart will create settings for strategic conversations that capitalize on those connections. Cross-pollination throughout the web results in organizations being more adaptive to a changing environment. Your role as a leader and facilitator is to multiply these conversational settings, ensuring all voices are heard.

Emotional Intelligence

Great leaders and facilitators exude authority, gentle strength, and a can-do spirit rooted in their emotional and spiritual core. This type of maturity is evident to groups. It elicits trust and leads to better functioning meetings. Facilitators who exude nervousness and anxiety infect the whole group with nervousness and anxiety. Calm, steady leaders enable the group to do its work. This calm directs attention away from the leaders to the group.

Much has been written in recent years about emotional intelligence, resilience, and mindfulness. Each term expresses an aspect of emotionally mature, spiritually-centered leadership that helps groups function well.

Reidan S. Nadler writes, "[Emotional Intelligence] can be defined in terms of understanding yourself, managing yourself, understanding others, and managing others" (*Leading with Emotional Intelligence,* p. 9). The best leaders and facilitators score high on emotional intelligence.

Emotional intelligence includes the ability to contain anxiety and recover after difficulties. When multiple demands and pressures confront a person, emotional intelligence is the quality in a person that exudes forbearance, patience, and confidence. Emotional intelligence draws power from the frontal cortex and tames the reptilian brain. Emotionally mature and resilient people catch hardballs with a soft glove. They catch the emotions that are thrown their way and field them with calm and finesse.

Mindfulness is a tool or discipline that helps us find our emotional and spiritual center. Methods for achieving mindfulness vary from one person to another. Some meditate. Others pray. Some take deep, relaxing breaths. Some close their eyes and imagine relaxing every muscle. Others visualize a mountain vista or gentle waves brushing the seashore. Many people combine several of these elements. Mindfulness slows the breathing and heart rate and calms jangled nerves.

Fortunately, emotional intelligence, resilience, and mindfulness can be learned. This chapter suggests eight qualities or practices to strengthen emotional intelligence. They include developing self-awareness, humor, empathy, and curiosity; physical exercise; telling stories of courage; living with gratitude, and incorporating play into your life. First, a story.

I was asked to facilitate a meeting of bicyclists and neighborhood advocates one week after the cycling death of a beloved city council member on a city street. Sid Tyler was struck and killed in a bike lane along Del Mar Boulevard, an arterial in Pasadena, California. Although the posted speed limit was thirty-five miles per hour, police estimated the hit-and-run driver was going fifty-five when he struck the beloved political leader. Mr. Tyler was not the first cyclist to be injured or killed by a motorist on Del Mar Boulevard. Its five wide lanes encouraged speeding.

I knew the forum would be heated, filled with anger, rage, grief, and fear. I knew the frustration with the Pasadena Department of Transportation was high. Some residents felt the City was unresponsive to the biking community's needs. As the facilitator, I knew that the meeting design needed to channel anger and pain in a productive direction. I needed to be at my emotional best, with a good supply of mindfulness and resilience.

So, I took a hike—literally. My home was mere minutes from hiking trails in the San Gabriel Mountains. Calling my two dogs, I hiked with Abbey and Troy up the steep trails, absorbing the beauty of sunlight on chaparral. As a Jesus follower, I prayed. I asked the Holy One for peace. Then I came down from the mountains.

I met with a small planning committee who decided to hold a strategy World Café (See *Large Group Planning Methods* for a description of the World Café method). We planned two sets of questions, each with three, twenty-minute rounds of conversation. The first question was, "How have biking accidents personally affected my life?"

During the World Café, participants shared stories of close calls and accidents, pain and anger. Because I was internally at peace, I was able to field the group's anger and pain. The format permitted deep sharing and gave everyone a voice. Although emotions ran high, the forum was respectful.

When the "harvest" of plenary comments came, the universality of experience was remarkable. No one seemed unscathed—everyone seemed to care. The need for and the challenge of redesigning Pasadena to be more biking and walking friendly was starkly evident.

Then we broke into the second cycle of conversations on the question, "What bold steps if fully implemented, would make Pasadena the safest biking community in California?" Again, we held three rounds of conversation in groups of four, followed by a 30-minute plenary harvest. This time, the group generated a series of strategic actions. They specified which streets should have biking paths with physical barriers and which streets needed reduced speeds. The group committed to building a coalition of pedestrian, biking, and neighborhood advocates that would keep their issues before the city government.

The group's anger transformed into action and hope that shaped the transportation plan and policies for the City of Pasadena in the following years.

My emotional and spiritual preparation of hiking in the mountains with my dogs had allowed me to remain mindful and calm in a space filled with angry, hurting people. What could have been a disastrous event was, instead, an experience of resilience and redemption.

Emotional intelligence, mindfulness, and resilience are learned behaviors. They can be perfected. Essential practices for building these leadership qualities include self-awareness, humor, empathy, curiosity, physical exercise, and telling stories of courage, living with gratitude, and incorporating play into your life.

Self-awareness begins the journey toward greater emotional intelligence. "Know thyself," wrote Socrates in *Phaedrus*. Know both your mind and heart. Hire a therapist. Invite someone to help you explore what makes you tick. Look inside to the motives, feelings, and attitudes that shape your behavior. Develop an awareness of your cultural makeup (See *Cultural Mindfulness and Radical Inclusion*). Recognize your privilege and power due to race, class, ethnicity, sex, gender identity, education, profession, marital status, national origin, and so on. Grow in resilience by knowing yourself.

Self-awareness also includes recognizing your emotions and containing them. Containment is different from repression. Containment means being aware of your emotions and not letting them control you. You both feel them and know that you can choose how to react to them. "Be angry, but do not sin," is a saying from Christian scripture. Feel your emotions powerfully but do not allow them to control your behavior. When we are aware of the powerful emotions inside us, we are more able to choose forbearance in the face of threat, compassion in the midst of fear, and respect for all in polarized times.

Next, embrace the power of **humor**, especially self-deprecating humor. Humor and laughter are the lubricants for smooth relationships. Closely related to humor are optimism and seeing the good in life rather than dwelling on what is wrong. Laughing at oneself brings humility and a sense that one is not the center of the universe. Laughter brings a sense of ease and delightful relaxation.

Resilience is built on a foundation of **empathy**. Empathy is the practice of imagining walking in another person's shoes. What might it be like to be a young black man in America walking down a street in a hoodie and realize people are afraid of you, whether you are enrolled at Harvard or not? What is it like to be thirteen, Latina, and incarcerated in a holding facility in the United States after having fled gang violence in Central America? What is it like to be a police officer breaking down the door of a suspected heroin den in the knowledge that AR-15s are now the weapon of choice? Emotionally mature folk use their empathy and imagination to feel the other's pain and joy.

Empathic people listen not only to the words but to the inner meanings and the emotional core of the other. As a privileged, white, professional, married, heterosexual American, I can never fully know the experience of a poor pregnant woman who struggles to make ends meet and keep her family intact, but I can try. I can listen. I can imagine. I can observe. I can be quiet and allow others to speak who know more than I.

Curiosity. Emotional intelligence is also rooted in curiosity. Inquire into subjects that are new to you. Develop a new hobby. Read a book.

Most importantly, ask questions. When our ancestors gathered around the campfire, and the conversation turned to the next day's activities, questions were central: What food supplies lay over the horizon? What will happen if we cross the sea? What if we plant this seed over there? What if we heat these rocks? By asking such questions, we discovered new lands and continents, wheat, rice, and barley on which civilization depends, and smelting iron from ore with which we crafted swords and plowshares.

Curiosity is central to our species. It is how we spread from the Great Rift Valley in Ethiopia to the farthest reaches of the globe. Curiosity inspired Albert Einstein to discover the Theory of Relativity, Neal Armstrong to walk on the moon, and Madame Curie to discover radioactivity.

Physical exercise strengthens our resilience. Facilitators need to have all eight cylinders firing. Our brains need energy and abundant oxygen. Regular exercise of the body, heart, and lungs makes the brain work better, faster, and with greater precision. It gives us a sense of agency and power.

Tell **stories of courage** and savor them. Emotional intelligence and resilience are dependent on remembering the previous perseverance and courage of both ourselves and others. The world is awash in stories of abuse, fear, and violence. While we must not turn our eyes away from suffering, we need stories of triumph in the face of darkness, courage in the face of fear, decency, and compassion in the face of hatred and intolerance to help us persevere.

One of the stories I rely on is that of my paternal grandmother, Agnes Smutny. Her mother killed herself when Grandma Smutny was nine-years-old. When the dustbowl and Great Depression assaulted her young family in Nebraska, they sold the farm and moved to a Czech community in Buhl, Idaho. Her husband, my grandfather, was intelligent when sober and abusive when drunk. The stories of his abusive behavior are not fit for print. Grandma endured and persevered.

Grandma Smutny courageously divorced her abusive husband while most of her children were still at home. She went back to school and became a licensed practical nurse. She brought good from even the bitter circumstances of her life by caring for people. She dressed wounds, emptied bedpans, and comforted the sick and dying. In her crusty way, she made compassion the center of her life. The stories from people grateful for her care abound. More than a decade after her death, she continues to inspire me when I need courage.

We need compelling stories like this, stories of courage overcoming circumstance. Stories of compassion in the face of fear. Stories of healing, hope, and beauty. When these stories become central to who we are, when we tell them again and again, they inspire us to be better leaders, better facilitators, and better human beings.

Live with gratitude, and you will deepen your well of resilience. When we give thanks for the people in our lives, the beauty around us, and the kindness of others, it is impossible to be sour. Gratitude rewires the brain. We move from negativity to hope. The thousand picky details we are prone to complain about fade away. Our hearts and minds fill with good things.

Today, at this writing, I'm grateful for free speech, the media, and the First Amendment. I'm grateful for the sun peeking over the horizon and filling the skies with ribbons of yellow, red, and orange. I'm grateful for the warmth of my wife's body, her humor, and her superb editing abilities. I'm grateful for my four wonderful granddaughters, my two puppy dogs, and the gift of writing. The list can go on and on. I notice as I express gratitude that I become happier, lighter, more generous.

Be grateful. Speak your gratitude out loud. Write everything you are grateful for on a sheet of paper or your computer. Your emotional intelligence will increase as you remember to give thanks for blessings in your life.

Play. I love to sit down on the floor with my three-year-old granddaughter and help her piece together picture puzzles. I love to tell silly stories, all untrue, like this one about our fictional cat that sipped gasoline from a pan under the car I was working on.

> I was changing the oil and fixing a quirky gas pump. Jezebel took one or two sips of gas then ran full speed into the house. It was terrible, the poor thing. She zipped from room to room. Up and down the stairs, then into the dining room. She scrambled up the dining room curtains and stopped. Teetering from the curtain rod, she fell eight feet to the floor and lay still. All was quiet. You ask, "Did she die?" No. She ran out of gas.

Playfulness comes in many forms. Dance, tease mildly and play games. Play with your pets. I have two dogs, Kate and Grace, who love to hike, chase squirrels in the backyard, and try to climb trees. They also love to hike. We play a game where they rocket down a path at full speed. When I whistle, they turn and rocket past me in the opposite direction. After a hundred yards, I signal again. They reverse and streak past again.

After a dozen times, they plunk down in the dirt, exhausted. Their smiling, happy faces fill me with joy.

So, play Scrabble, Monopoly, ping pong, or video games, as long as you do not take them too seriously. Play hide-and-seek with your children or grandchildren. Take a class in ballroom dancing. Organize a poker party. Watch *Black Panther, Groundhog Day, or The Runaway Bride.* Play and laugh. If you can delight in the joy of play, your capacity to bear with the darker side of life will strengthen. You will sense a difference and others will notice as well.

Building self-awareness, empathy, and humor; telling stories of courage, exercising, developing curiosity, expressing gratitude, and being playful will not only strengthen your emotional intelligence, but they will also change your life. You will have a greater capacity for coping with loss when it comes. You'll discover that working through conflict is easier. You will enjoy life more. As a facilitator, you will bring joy and energy to your work.

The Art of Listening Well

Everyone can benefit from honing listening skills: parents, colleagues, teachers, counselors, supervisors, friends, and facilitators. I am indebted to John Savage for teaching me many of the core skills in this chapter. John Savage is a United Methodist pastor and clinical psychologist. His book, *Listening and Caring Skills: A Guide for Groups and Leaders,* and workshops changed my life and are the inspiration behind this chapter. I am a better listener, parent, husband, and trainer because of him.

Using listening skills in tandem with an empathetic spirit builds trust with the groups you lead and facilitate. If you are a consultant, you will be better able to serve your clients' needs. If you are an executive or chair of a board or committee, your group will function better and have higher participation. Good listening strengthens the effectiveness of *all* leaders. Whether in public service, business, or the nonprofit world, listening well improves your ability to understand the people with whom you work and helps meetings thrive. As an added benefit, listening well improves your relationships with family, friends, and neighbors.

The following pages describe and illustrate seven listening skills. Enjoy reading about them and incorporating them into your life and work. However, the best way to learn listening skills is to take a course or find a coach, and practice.

Paraphrase

One of the most frequently used listening skills is the act of reflecting to the speaker in your own words what you heard the person say. Paraphrase summarizes the speaker's content. Its purpose is to check out your initial understanding of what a person wants to communicate. It is often called "reflective listening."

Paraphrase has two components: the stem and the restatement of the speaker's content by using key words or phrases. Examples of stems:

"You're saying that . . ."

"What I hear you saying is that . . ."

"If I hear you right, you are . . ."

"Let me say what I'm hearing . . ."

A key word or words from the speaker follows the stem. These are the nouns, verbs, and adjectives you heard. Here is an example:

Speaker: I've been to four stores this afternoon and still haven't found the dress shirt I want. It is frustrating. Do you have any idea how much time I have wasted looking for that blasted gift?

Listener: You're saying you've been to a lot of stores and wasted a whole lot of time. You wonder whether I realize how much time it took.

Speaker: Yes and no. I want you to know how hard I tried and that I am frustrated. That is all. What is for dinner?

Paraphrase tests whether the words you received are the speaker's intended meaning. As the listener, you are checking out whether you got the content and meaning correct. Another example:

Speaker: I am trying to explain to you what I mean by paraphrase and hope that by giving you an example, you will understand the power of this skill.

Listener: You're giving me an explanation and example of paraphrase, and you hope it helps. You want me to know how powerful paraphrasing is for effective communication.

Do not repeat back what was said, word for word. Parroting backfires.

Speaker: "I said that I was angry!"

Listener: "You said you were angry!"

Speaker: "Yes!!!!!"

Parroting is a sign of an amateur listener and can be heard as mockery. Instead, use some of the key words and vary the stem.

Creative Questions

Curiosity and questions are intrinsic to being human. From the days we first learned to speak, we ask questions. "Why, Mommy?" "Why, Daddy?" "Where do butterflies fly?" "What is the moon made of?" A child's natural curiosity is essential for learning about life. No less for adults.

Creative questions are based on the content of what a speaker has said. They help the listener gain more information. With the right questions, a listener develops a more nuanced understanding of what is being communicated. Here is an example:

Speaker: "When I come home after a busy day, I need five minutes to discombobulate before I can engage in conversation. Just five minutes and then I can chat."

Listener: "You need a break?"

Speaker: "Yep. Just a small break and I'll be fine."

Another example:

Speaker: "The retreat was successful in lots of ways. We had lots of people present and great diversity. However, the outcomes were vague. I wish the facilitator had helped us focus more. We wasted time. Next retreat I attend, I'd like to see more focus on results."

Listener: "The results were hazy? How so?"

Speaker: "I wanted us to develop a work plan. "

Listener: "What would you like to see in the plan?"

Speaker: "I'd like to describe the next steps, the timeframe, and who the responsible party will be. This is urgent. We're facing a funding deadline.

Listener: "What's the deadline?"

Speaker: The end of next week and I am stressed about it.

Notice how much more detail the speaker disclosed because of the questions that built on one another. Creative questions invite the speaker to go deeper. They welcome further reflection and insight into the mind of the speaker. They are a simple but powerful tool. Another example:

Speaker: I am concerned that my confidentiality will not be protected in this conversation. I am not willing to go further until I am protected.

Listener: You're not sure you want to talk? What behavior in me would help you feel safer?

Speaker: The assurance that what we discuss will be treated as a sacred trust.

Listener: Is a verbal assurance enough?

Speaker: I believe so.

Listener: Is there anything else that would help?

Speaker: Yes. That we promise to keep these discussions only between us. Then I can trust you.

Notice the series of creative questions again. Each one builds on the previous question. In this case, each question strengthens the bonds of trust. The power of creative questions is that it enables the speaker to tell his or her unique story. Frequently, free information is given on topics you did not ask about. New avenues of inquiry become possible.

A particular type of creative question helps when speakers distort reality. Distortions are common in communication because we regularly color and spin what we say. Most of us color our communications to depict the world and us the way we want them to be.

Words such as every, never, always, continuously, forever, never, nobody, everyone, and everywhere are nearly always a distortion. They are absolutes.

"Everybody knows I am the best."

"We always behave the best of all nations in the world."

"No one has ever worked as hard as I."

"I always wash the dishes. You never wash the dishes."

"We never accomplish anything in these meetings."

As my mother-in-law is fond of saying (tongue in cheek), "Never use absolutes." These hyperbolic statements distort the truth. The best way to respond to an absolute statement is to ask a creative question. For example:

Speaker: "We've never seen an economy as productive as the one we have now."

Listener: "Never?"

Speaker: "Absolutely never!"

Listener: "How about the post-war boom?"

Speaker: "Well, yeah. I suppose."

Another example:

Parent: "You never clean your room. You always leave it a total mess."

Teen: "Never? How about the time we cleaned it together?"

The purpose of checking out the distortion word is to bring the speaker more in line with reality. The best response is to ask a creative question when you hear statements such as, "You're never home." "He always puts colleagues down." "Everybody is against me."

Ask your question using the distorted word: "Never?" "Anyone?" "Everybody?" These questions challenge the speaker to correct the distortion. Follow up with another creative question:

Speaker: "No one thinks I'm a buffoon!"

Listener: "No one? Not one person? What makes you think no one thinks you're a bozo?"

Speaker: "Well, there might be a few."

Listener: "A few?"

Speaker: "Okay. More than a few."

Incorporating the absolute word and asking a creative question invites the speaker to dial it down. The speaker's words will become closer to reality.

As wonderful as creative questions can be, the wrong question can block or stop a conversation. Poor listeners commonly ask questions that are off subject, poorly timed, or invasive. They seem empathy-challenged, uncaring, or unskilled. Most often, this happens when a painful subject comes up.

Speaker: "I am so sad about the recent gun shootings in our neighborhood."

Listener: "Have you thought about the good things happening in our world?"

Ouch. End of conversation.

Speaker: "I am still at a loss for words when I think about the death of my partner."

Listener: "You were lucky to have a partner. Have you thought of all the people out there still looking for someone special?

Ouch. Cold silence.

Good listeners stay quiet at times like this, or, when the time is right, ask a simple question or respond with a simple sentence such as:

"You're sad, aren't you? I can only imagine."

"I imagine you're ticked! Am I right?"

"Your loss sounds profound."

Good listeners bear the emotion. They contain their reaction and focus on the other's feeling words instead of running from them. When appropriate, they may reveal their emotional state:

"I'm saddened by the shootings, as well.

"My anger gets stirred up, too."

"Your loss breaks my heart."

When responding to emotional statements, do not use the word "must," as in "You must be sad." Remember, you do not know exactly how the other feels. Assumptions are dangerous. It is better to say something such as "I imagine you're really sad." This gives the other space and does not impose your feelings on him or her.

In summary, creative questions can generate free information without asking, fill in holes with missing information, and correct distortion. Creative questions are an essential tool for listening well.

Perception Check

Perception check tests your hunch regarding another person's emotional state. The skill has four steps: observing the speaker's behavioral clues, identifying a feeling, making a tentative statement, and asking a question. All four steps combine to make up perception check—a skill experienced as caring.

1. Look and listen for clues that express emotion. The face is the most frequent source for locating emotions. Changes in eye shape, skin tone and tension, smiles and frowns are non-verbal ways we communicate emotions. Emotional messages are also communicated through changes in tone of voice, body movements, whether a person is slouched or has arms folded, is tearing up, or gesturing with strong movements

in the arms and hands. Clenched jaws and rigid limbs send powerful emotional messages, too.

2. Make an internal guess at the feelings that have been expressed but not named. There are hundreds of names for emotions. The most common ones are anger, fear, disgust, joy, happiness, sadness, surprise, excitement, and contempt.

3. Make a tentative statement using a stem such as:

    "I notice that . . ."

    "I'm guessing you might be feeling . . ."

    "I wonder if you're feeling. . ."

4. Complete the above sentence by expressing your hunch of what the other person or group is feeling.

    "I'm wondering if you're sad with what's happening at work."

    "I notice that your voice seems strained. I'm guessing you feel hurried?

    "You're smiling. I'm guessing this is a funny moment for you. Yes?"

A skilled facilitator can use perception check in a group when emotions are running high.

> "Okay. Let's touch base with the mood of the group. I'm guessing the group is worn out and needs a break. Am I correct?"
>
> "Friends, let's slow down. I'm noticing there's some tension in the air and some frustration. Am I on target?"

One or more creative questions can follow the perception check:

"What issue seems to be causing the tension?"

"What am I missing here?"

"What needs to be addressed first before we can move on?"

"What question, if addressed, would help us move our conversation to the next level?"

One danger with a perception check is that it can be perceived as invasive. In a low trust environment, emotion words need to have low intensity. For example, in a setting of low trust where emotions are high, and you sense frustration and anger, use the emotion words "stressed" and "concerned" instead of "angry" and "frustrated." The use of less intense emotion reduces the threat of being invasive. It demonstrates respect and empathy.

Examples of feeling words with different intensities:

Happy: comfortable, at ease, joyful.

Sad: blue, sorry, unhappy.

Angry: hurt, stressed, upset, concerned.

Energized: excited, engaged.

Bored: tired, unengaged, fed up, worn-out.

Perception check is one of the most empathic listening skills. When used properly, a skilled facilitator can help a group stay in tune with its collective emotions and work more productively. When used with individuals, it is a wonderful, caring tool. Use it wisely.

Direct Expression of Feelings

The purpose of direct expression of feelings is to identify and name your emotional state. For example, "I feel a sense of pride in what the group has accomplished."

When the leader or facilitator expresses his or her emotional state, usually followed by a creative question, the group can get a sense of its mood.

"I'm feeling good about making it through that complicated conversation. Wow. We did it. How are all of you feeling?"

Expressing your emotional state as a facilitator may help your group recognize its emotional state. Groups may be angry, frustrated, bored, sad, excited, energized, hurt, confused, eager, calm, or centered.

For example, I facilitated an all-day transportation summit in Seattle in which the focus was to strengthen how seniors and persons with disabilities find transportation. The day began with lots of energy. The morning was dedicated to a World Café (See the chapter, *Large Group Planning Methods*) centered on people sharing what they typically experience when seeking transportation. By late morning, the group had produced some common themes.

By early afternoon, my energy was waning. Nonetheless, the group needed to stay focused and energized because it had another two hours to meet. The most important part of the meeting lay ahead — the group energy needed to remain high as we turned to problem-solving.

I decided to share my emotional state followed by a series of creative questions. I said, "I'm feeling a little fatigue. My tummy is full, and I'm sleepy. How's the group doing? How's your energy? Are you ready to go again?" The group responded, "Let's do it."

The act of directly expressing my emotional state and asking the group about its own helped re-energize everyone.

On another occasion, I worked with a church group in Los Angeles that was closing its doors after 130 years of existence. Its membership had dwindled to 20 members, many of them in their 80s. The governing board invited me to help it decide what to do with its church property. They wanted to make sure that something good came from the death of their congregation.

As the facilitator, I decided to use a technique called *1-2-4-All* to help the group distill its ideas for the property (See the chapter, *Liberating Structures*). Each person took one minute to write down on a piece of paper what he or she thought should happen to the property. Then I invited church members to choose another person and, in groups of two, share all their ideas. Next, I asked them to form groups of four and take six minutes to share. Then we reconvened in a whole-group session. People shared highlights of their conversations in popcorn style. (Popcorn style is when either individuals or a representative from a small group reports out one item to share with the larger group. The ideas pop up from individual to individual—popcorn style.)

Participants shared ideas such as selling the church to a younger congregation, developing an investment fund that supported a mission, and seeing if a local nonprofit working on affordable housing might want the building free of charge.

I expected the group to be sad and depressed. I, myself, had come into the meeting feeling somewhat anxious and sad. Closing a congregation can be a depressing event for the people who remain active.

However, I did not sense sadness in the group as the event progressed. Indeed, I sensed relief and energy. I decided to express my own emotions followed by a creative question.

> Me: "I'm saddened by this decision to close. I'm wondering how the group is doing?"

What I got back was, "No, we're sick and tired of being sad. It's time to move on. We'll be sad on our last Sunday, and we'll all be relieved because we've been dealing with sad for years! Let's decide what we're going to do!" Wow. That was the farthest response from what I expected. I was glad I asked.

Expressing my emotions directly, followed by a question, helped in several ways. It helped me correct my assumption about the group. It helped the group focus on the task at hand. It helped them identify the complex emotional journey they were on and, I believe, assisted them in preparing emotionally for when the date of the closing arrived.

Here are some more examples of direct expression of feelings by a facilitator, followed by a creative question:

> "I'm confused where the group wants to head. Does someone want to summarize where we are?"

> "I'm feeling a little defensive. What do I need to hear from you to make sure this meeting stays on track? What am I missing?"

> "I'm feeling good about how the day concluded. How are you feeling?"

> "I'm feeling tense. How about we take a five-minute break and all of us catch our breath?"

Direct expression of feelings is a tool that helps groups and facilitators function well. Groups have collective emotions. These emotions shift and change depending on what is being discussed, the time of day and, especially, the difficulty of the topic. A skilled facilitator recognizes these emotional moods as well as his or her emotional state and responds accordingly.

Fogging

Fogging is a listening skill used when facing criticism. Responding well to critical comments is one of the most difficult listening skills to learn and most useful. Most of us respond to criticism by attacking, criticizing back or going quiet. None of these gives productive results. This is true in marriages, international relations, labor contract negotiations, and when facilitating polarized meetings. Defensiveness, counterattacks, and extended silence go nowhere fast.

> "You're being defensive."
>
> "No, I'm not. You seem defensive."
>
> "I do? No way. What's your problem?"

The purpose of fogging is to offer no hard resistance to your critic.

Speaker: You're being defensive."

Listener: "I have been known to feel defensive."

Speaker: "I wish you could hurry things up and get this group moving."

Listener: "I could do a better job of making things move along."

Fogging is called fogging because it is like hitting a fog bank. There is no rebound from striking a hard surface. A bank of thin vapor swallows the harsh fist of criticism. The listener refuses to fight back.

Fogging agrees with anything in the statement the critic makes that is true for you. When fogging, agree only with what is true for you. Do not compromise your integrity. Use the skill truthfully.

Fogging works with several different stems:

> "That's right."
>
> "You're probably right."
>
> "I guess you're right."
>
> "You could be right."

"You're right."

"There's truth in what you say."

These statements generate fog. They communicate you won't play the game of criticism and its endless cycle of back-and-forth. The soft contours of fog replace the hard edges of criticism.

Critic: "You annoy me with your poor facilitation skills."

Fog: "I could be better at facilitation."

Critic: "Have you ever been trained to run a nonprofit?"

Fog: "I could always use more training."

Critic: "Have you ever ended a meeting on time?"

Fog: "I could definitely pay more attention to ending meetings on time."

Critic: "I'm unwilling to endure such poor leadership."

Fog: "Poor leadership is hard to endure."

Notice how the fogging statement agrees with only what you believe is true. As you listen to the critical statement, it is not difficult to find something with which you agree. For example, you are a manager and in a conflict with an employee. The dialogue goes something like this:

Employee: "We're not going to meet our performance metrics this month because we're not getting sufficient direction from you. Can't you step up? Why aren't you giving us any guidance?"

Manager: "It's true our performance metrics are down."

Employee: "It's your lack of leadership and all those irrelevant meetings you attend."

Manager: "I do attend lots of meetings, and some are not directly relevant to our performance."

Employee: "Let me also say, you did not meet with us last week."

Manager: "You're right. I didn't. That could be part of the problem. Shall we set up a meeting for this week and go over our performance?"

Fogging is rarely used in isolation. Usually, it is used in combination with other listening skills such as creative questions, perception check, and paraphrase. In each example, the fogging step is tucked among creative questions.

Retreat attendee: "I think you need to move our meeting along faster."

Facilitator: "It's true we could move a little faster. Shall we finish up this item or go on to the next right now? What would the group like to do?"

Retreat attendee: "We have not heard from all voices. Could you pay more attention to those who haven't yet spoken? You seem to call on only the loudest people."

Facilitator: "You're right. I could pay more attention to people who haven't spoken. How would you like me to proceed? Who hasn't spoken?"

Professional facilitators and organizational leaders are frequently called upon to help during an open conflict. When tempers are high, combining fogging with other skills can be helpful. For example, when discussing highly polarized topics like immigration, gun violence, or reproductive rights, fogging at the right time can reduce the tension in the group and help the group engage in respectful dialogue.

Speaker: "The other side has no respect for those of us who support gun rights."

Facilitator: "We could always use more respect. How would you like to be respected?"

Speaker: "I want to be heard instead of dismissed as a reactionary."

Facilitator: "What would you suggest we do to hear all perspectives?"

Speaker: "Give us time to prepare what we want to say."

Facilitator: "By giving you time to prepare, you'd feel more respected, am I right?"

Speaker: "Yes."

Facilitator: "How much time do you need?"

Speaker: "Ten minutes, please."

Facilitator: "Would both sides like to take ten minutes?"

Speakers: "Yes. That would be great."

Facilitator: "Let's take a break and in ten minutes reconvene. Then the sides can speak for five minutes each. Would that help everyone to feel more respected?"

All: "Yes."

Note that the interaction begins with fogging and is followed by a series of creative questions and a perception check. Remember that fogging is naming the truth in another person's criticism. Name only what is true for you. When you incorporate fogging in your listening skill toolkit, you will be better equipped to cope with criticism, difficult people, and polarized settings.

Negative Inquiry

Negative inquiry is another listening skill to use when facing criticism. The goal of this skill is to turn your critic into your coach rather than your opponent. Negative inquiry is typically used in combination with fogging and other listening skills. The essence of negative inquiry is to ask your critic to point out specific behaviors that are upsetting him or her.

Criticism tends to come at us in generalizations, with specific behaviors rarely identified. Changing behavior appropriately is impossible if we do not know what specifically the critic is criticizing.

When facilitating meetings, leaders and consultants may receive criticism. Maybe a member of the group insists you are running a poor meeting. However, your critic does not name any specific behaviors that bother him or her. You can only guess at what they may be. Negative inquiry invites the critic to name specific behaviors that he or she wants you to change if you so choose.

Negative inquiry can be useful when chairing meetings, leading retreats, or hosting a community forum. It is most helpful for consultants whose business is dependent on good relationships.

A few years ago, I had worked hard preparing a proposal with an agency. I was one of two consultants they interviewed to facilitate their strategic plan. I had produced what I thought was a well-thought-out proposal, very detailed and thorough. I did not get the contract and had no idea why. I called the executive director and asked if he would be willing to teach me how I could do a better job with future clients. He agreed.

Using Negative Inquiry I asked,

"What specific concerns did the steering committee have about my proposal?"

"The length of time it would take to complete."

"What concerned you about the length?"

"We had a deadline of June 1 for a completed project. Your plan wouldn't be completed until September 1, and couldn't meet our deadline."

"Were there other concerns?"

"Yes. We thought your proposal duplicated efforts we had already completed."

"Could you tell me what those efforts were?

"We'd already completed an environmental scan, and you had us do a SWOT Analysis all over again."

"Is there anything else that concerned you?"

"No. We were impressed by the thoroughness of your proposal. It just didn't meet our needs to move quickly."

I learned a great deal about why I missed the mark on the consulting proposal. I learned to be more careful in listening to clients. In the initial interview, I had missed how important a brief process was. By using

Negative Inquiry, I turned the rejection of my consulting proposal into a learning experience.

The structure of Negative Inquiry is to ask questions of your critic that fill in missing details.

Here are a few examples:

Critic: "You are a very poor facilitator."

Listener: "I understand that you think I could be a better facilitator. What specifically do you wish I would improve?"

Critic: "You got us started fifteen minutes late. We wasted time socializing."

Listener: "Is there anything else about my facilitation that concerns you?"

Critic: "You didn't welcome everyone. How can you start a meeting and not greet everyone?"

Listener: "Anything else?"

Critic: "No. That's it."

Negative Inquiry has the added benefit of calming its user. When criticized, we often feel defensive and under attack. We tend to act out of fear, anger, and the desire to fight or flee. Negative Inquiry calms the nerves. It turns the cycle of criticism and counter-criticism into a learning experience.

Story Listening

Telling stories is at the center of what makes us human. Children tell stories. Teens tell stories. Adults tell stories. Especially important to meeting facilitators and leaders, groups tell stories.

All types of organizations, businesses, and coalitions tell stories. They have narratives about their founding, ups, downs, successes, and mistakes. Their stories arc from accomplishment to disappointment to revitalization. Groups have stories of humble beginnings to great success to decline and renewal.

Embedded within an organization's narrative may be undisclosed loss, triumph, paralysis, hope, and pride. Listening to the deeper, inner meanings of a group's story is an advanced listening skill. Once you grasp the power of story listening, your listening will take a turn toward greater depth and effectiveness.

I'll begin with a story. Years ago, I facilitated a planning retreat in California for a merchant's association. The business group was on a death curve, and the city's senior planner wanted help revitalizing it. Only a handful of long-time Caucasian business owners remained active.

However, downtown was experiencing growth spurred by new businesses owned by recent Chinese immigrants. In-fill housing was being built close to downtown. The challenge was that only a couple of the new Chinese businesses had joined the business group.

I met with the association's board and began listening to their collective narrative. I asked how they got started. I asked about the founding leaders and the organization's priorities when they organized. I asked about moments of crisis and times of innovation and success. I asked when they were most vibrant and when they went into decline.

Here's the most important part: I listened to their inner story—the highly symbolic and metaphorical meaning of their journey together. What I heard was repeated short cycles of innovation followed by much longer periods of decline and relative inactivity. The group's foundation story, its creation story, if you will, was a story of aggressively reaching out to businesses. Founding board members went door-to-door, begging everyone they met to join the association and help turn around what had been a declining downtown. I learned they handed out flyers and business cards for the business group in every gathering place and business. They were outwardly focused and mission-driven.

Once up and running with dozens of businesses participating, they hired a part-time executive director. She was good at organizing monthly informational meetings on various topics. She was excellent at expressing their viewpoint before the city government. She was a pro in developing their marketing and promotions strategy.

However, board members stopped reaching out to new businesses. They stopped. Instead, they came to monthly meetings, participated in board meetings, and attended public hearings for developers' entitlements. When the demographics of the community began to shift with an influx of Mandarin-speaking residents and businesses, they still focused on serving their long-time businesses. They did not craft new outreach strategies suitable for their rapidly changing community. Silently, I noted the patterns.

I recommended to the board that they convene a large group of community stakeholders: business owners, the merchant association's staff and board, city planning staff, city manager, and a couple of elected officials. I recommended a Timeline Exercise. (See the chapter, *The Art of Coming to Terms with Organizational History.*)

The group that showed up for the event was majority Euro-American. The purpose of the Timeline Exercise is to make explicit the inner, usually unconscious, story of a group and help the group discover new energy and strategic focus. It proved effective.

The group recorded key moments in their history on a long piece of butcher paper taped along one wall. The paper had headings spanning their 25-year history in five-year intervals: 1990, 1995, 2000, 2005, 2010, and 2015.

I invited them to tell stories of their founding: who led, who worked hard, and what they did. I invited them to describe how they reached out. They wrote the information on the butcher paper. They recorded what the economy was doing over the time of their existence, as well as changes in political leadership within their city and the country. I invited them to recollect changes in the neighborhoods surrounding the downtown and when new immigrant communities began to arrive in significant numbers. They recorded twenty-five years of collective history on the timeline.

Once the timeline was fleshed out, I asked what they noticed. What patterns did they see? What insights did they have? One after another, the business owners said:

> "We used to get out in the community."

> "When we started, we worked hard on getting new members."

> "When we hired Francine, we started to depend on her to do everything. We stopped being salespeople for the organization."

> "When the 2008 Great Recession hit, we went into serious decline."

I asked, "When you look at your timeline, what does it tell you about who you need to be going forward? What insights do you have?"

"We need to take some risks."

"We need to be as aggressive as when we began."

"We need to get off our duffs and reach out to all the new businesses."

"We need to hire a part-time, bilingual staff member who speaks English and Mandarin who can help us reach out and listen to the new Chinese businesses."

What I heard during both my initial interview and the Timeline Exercise was a repeated story of triumph and decline. Whenever the association was focused outward, it discovered energy. When it stopped reaching out to newcomers, it sped down the slippery slope of irrelevance.

Hearing their inner story and helping the group collectively hear it led the business association and city into a new period of innovation. After a year of work reaching out, going door-to-door, and hiring a part-time staff member who spoke the language of the new immigrant community, the group began to grow again. They developed an aggressive bilingual marketing and promotions plan. Most significantly, the association's leaders moved from despair to hope and became culturally more diverse. Their changing neighborhood was no longer a threat but an opportunity for growth.

Story listening is a transformational tool. It recognizes that a group's narrative profoundly shapes their behavior. Skilled facilitators can help a group discover the stories out of which they act and use those stories as clues to the future. They can make a lasting difference in the life and health of an agency, neighborhood group, business association, or congregation.

The listening skills described in this chapter can help you be a better listener, leader, facilitator, friend, and partner. They are learned, not inherited—learned through repeated practice. At first, learning new listening skills can feel awkward, like the first time you rode a bike. With lots of practice and time, however, listening well will become natural.

Structuring an Agenda

I will cut to the chase. You are reading this book to help you facilitate meetings well and learn techniques to include all voices. The most common meetings are the weekly staff meetings, the work groups we attend or run, and the community meetings that blanket the landscape of the globe. True, we also participate in conferences, annual staff meetings, and summits, but these are rare and occur only a few times a year. The chapter, *Large Group Planning Methods*, describes several designs for these larger, less frequent meetings. This chapter explores basic practices to help your normal, everyday meetings thrive.

Let us begin by forming an agenda. I will outline the steps.

Listening

A skilled facilitator drafts an agenda by first listening. Listen to your work team or planning group. If you are constructing an agenda alone, listen to those who will attend the meeting. As you listen, collect the issues and questions you believe should be discussed. Consider possible outcomes and the process for reaching them. Constructing an effective agenda is a dynamic, not linear, process.

Choosing the right design for your meeting and constructing an agenda should be based on answers to these questions:

- What issues do you hope to discuss?
- What questions, if answered, best advance what you hope to accomplish?
- What specific outcomes are you hoping will emerge?

- What meeting design will achieve your goals and engage all voices and perspectives?
- Will any topics evoke powerful emotions or be polarizing?
- How much time is available?
- How might the meeting begin in a way that helps people focus on the agenda at hand?
- What habits or guidelines for group behavior would you like to see?
- How might the room layout be arranged for best process and outcomes?
- What accommodations are needed to include persons with special needs?
- How might the meeting results be best recorded?
- How will the group and facilitator receive feedback on what went well and what did not?

Agenda Drafting

Assuming you have listened well, it is time to choose a meeting design and draft the agenda based on your answers to the above questions. A weekly check-in staff meeting with less than a dozen people will have a different agenda than a three-day conference with one-thousand people present.

Whichever design you choose, the best meeting agendas share common elements:

- Welcome
- Introductions
- Becoming fully present
- Ground rules
- Review of the meeting agenda
- Issues, questions, and process
- Clarifying outcomes and summarizing next steps
- Evaluation

Welcome. Every meeting should begin with a welcome. An upbeat, can-do spirit works best for most groups. Conflicted, tired, and impatient participants especially need to sense confidence and optimism in their facilitator: "Let's get started. We can do this. Let's get to work."

State the meeting's purpose in a clear voice and minimum words:

> "We're here to draft our department's asking budget for the fiscal year beginning January 1."

> "We're here to plan a summit on climate change that will result in a clear public policy strategy."

> "We have twenty minutes to establish ground rules that will guide our behavior for the next six months."

Introductions. Introductions vary according to the group's size, purpose, and familiarity. Even a group of hundreds can experience energy in a meeting with the right questions. At tables or in small groups, have participants share answers to these questions:

- Give your name and where you live.
- Where would you be if you were not at this meeting?
- Name a hope for today's event.

You might think a small group of co-workers who have worked together for years need no introductions. However, try these questions at a monthly meeting and see how much they enliven your group:

- Give your first name. Name one thing that is going well in your life.
- Give your name, tell who named you, and where your grandparents were born.

I facilitated a networking workshop for seventy-five transportation engineers, people not necessarily known as touchy-feely or talkative. During introductions, I asked them to form pairs. I said, "After you give your name, take two minutes each to describe the coolest project you designed as a child." Wow. The room erupted into a cacophony of gadget boasting. Engineer personalities turned into a verbal circus. The right question is like a lever that moves the world.

Becoming fully present. Facilitators cannot know in advance what is going on in the lives of participants. People may feel rushed, preoccupied with family, elated at a child's achievement, worried about paying bills or concerned about recent news. Everyone brings something: low expectations, high expectations, desire for a short meeting, hope for great outcomes. To become fully present and centered, they need to separate from their baggage.

A period of silence and deep breathing can accomplish this. For religious groups, a prayer. For others, use a guided meditation in which people are invited to relax their muscles and visualize a place of beauty. Another approach is to form pairs and briefly answer questions such as, "What did you have to give up to be here today?" or "If you were not here, what would you be doing?" Then, say something like, "Now, I invite all of you to set aside whatever was on your mind when you arrived. Those dirty dishes or that unfinished project will still be there for you to pick up when you leave. For now, be fully present to each other and to what we are doing here."

Ground rules. I once thought ground rules did not need to be repeated at every meeting of a group who knew each other well. I was wrong. Reviewing ground rules near the beginning of each meeting, even briefly, reinforces respectful behavior. Far from a waste of time, reviewing ground rules builds respectful meetings and organizations.

My favorite ground rules are the RESPECTFUL Communication Guidelines created by Eric Law and described in the chapter, *The Art of Ground Rules*. Use them or something similar. You can invite the group to form ground rules from scratch, perhaps seeding the group with a couple of suggestions. If you introduce an already written set of ground rules to a new group, dedicate plenty of time explaining each one and giving an example for how each rule or guideline can be used.

Review of the meeting agenda. Inviting participants to review the draft agenda near the beginning of the meeting and asking if they have ways to strengthen it can build ownership. Say, "Let's review the agenda. Is there anything we should add? Any suggestions to improve it?" By testing the waters with a draft agenda and asking a question such as "What suggestions do you have for strengthening this agenda?" your meeting attendees will help you build a better agenda.

Issues, Questions, and Process. The heart of every meeting is its issues or questions, its goals, and a process to achieve those goals. The best meeting agendas have a logical sequence for each subject:

Issue → Goal → Process

I prefer to frame issues as questions that need answering. The chapter, *The Art of Creative Questions,* describes how to frame questions that engage, energize, and inspire. Listing agenda items as phrases instead of questions can result in confusion and ambiguity. Imagine a staff meeting in which items for discussion are listed on the agenda in the following way:

1. Human Relations Software
2. Work Place Safety
3. Long Term Employee Celebration

Most of us have organized agenda items this way. The problem with the format is that it does not frame the issues in a meaningful way for discussion. Based on the information provided above, participants do not know:

1. What aspect of Human Relations software will you discuss? Is it a complaint session about the old software? Is it a plea for the HR and IT departments to work harder? Is it an information item about newly acquired software?
2. Is the item on workplace safety a report on accidents? Notification of an Excellence Award from OSHA? Will you focus on best practices or solicit ideas on improvements from employees?
3. Will the discussion focus on last year's celebration party? Alternatively, will you discuss certificates and types of gift cards for this year's long-term employees?

As you can see, participants have little idea from the agenda what they are expected to think about, discuss, and propose. This agenda is a roadmap for wandering in the wilderness.

The best meetings use open-ended questions in which the answer is not yet known. They provide content that invites creativity, concrete answers, goals, and next steps. They list the purpose of the topic. Is it to share information, develop solutions, or reach a decision? The first time I tried this and saw what a difference it makes, I felt like the tagline in the old V-8 tomato juice commercial, "I could have had a V-8!" The meeting was better in ways that are hard to describe.

Notice the difference between the above agenda items and those listed below. Each example below would be effective in establishing clarity and momentum in an agenda:

- What Human Relations software shall we recommend to the CEO?
- What steps and timeframe for implementing the new HR software shall we craft?
- How might our warehouses implement best safety practices in our industry by the end of 2020?
- How shall we celebrate long-term employees?
- What gifts shall we give to employees with 20+ years with the company?

If the goal is to brainstorm an issue, the agenda should say so and include the process.

- Brainstorm: What gifts shall we give to employees with 20+ years with the company?

If you want to use a stakeholder summit to strengthen workplace safety in warehouses, state it as a question and include the proposed meeting design.

- How might our warehouses implement the best safety practices in our industry by the end of 2020? We will hold a ninety-minute World Café of three twenty-minute rounds, followed by a thirty-minute harvest to discuss this question. The Human Relations Department will issue a summary of recommendations by 4:00 p.m. next Thursday, the 5th.

Note that the second example includes a time frame, deadline, and responsible party. Establishing a deadline and naming a responsible party for next steps adds clarity. Giving a time frame forces the facilitator to think about the meeting in a disciplined way and helps establish realistic expectations for the length of the meeting. Framing the amount of time for the agenda item has the added benefit of helping groups adhere to a schedule. When the time draws short, the facilitator can remind participants that time is nearly up.

Packing too much into a short time frame results in a meeting disaster and frustrated people. Facilitators tend to underestimate the amount of time an agenda item will take. Multiply the number of people in the group by the number of minutes you expect each to speak on a topic (10 people x 3 minutes = 30 minutes).

If the meeting's purpose is to reach a decision, state the method you will use. As the facilitator, you might say, "By the end of our meeting, I plan to take a vote. We'll decide by a simple majority." In groups that function by consensus, you might say, "After discussing this item for forty-five minutes, I will see if the group is ready to decide. If you need more time to reach a consensus, we'll decide then how much more time we need. Okay?"

Clarifying outcomes and summarizing next steps. Summarizing key decisions, clarifying outcomes, and naming the next steps increases meeting effectiveness. As the facilitator, you might ask the group to detail the outcomes and next steps, or you might summarize them. The chapter, *The Art of Recording Meetings,* describes "graphic recording," a method of visually capturing and summarizing a meeting's content. An effective way to increase clarity in some settings is by asking what items need to be on the next meeting's agenda based on the day's outcomes.

Evaluation. The purpose of an evaluation is to teach both the group and the facilitator what went well in the meeting, what needs strengthening, and how to do better the next time. It should not be merely a way to ventilate or tear down. Useful evaluations ask questions that improve your meetings and elicit constructive feedback. Design an evaluation using "appreciative questions" such as these:

- What went well in the meeting for you?
- What needed strengthening?

- What in the physical space and room set-up worked well? What needed changing?
- In what ways did the meeting design help? What would you suggest for improvements?
- What ideas do you have for strengthening the experience for all participants the next time this group meets?

Agenda Checklist

Now, let us assemble the whole kit and caboodle with an agenda checklist:

- ☐ Listen to Planning Team or Participants
- ☐ Draft Meeting Invitation
- ☐ Draft Agenda
- ☐ Send out Reports, Minutes, Articles, and Draft Agenda
- ☐ Set-up Meeting Room
- ☐ Welcome
- ☐ Introductions
- ☐ Becoming Fully Present: Icebreaker or Meditation or Both
- ☐ Agenda Review and Adoption
- ☐ Ground Rules
- ☐ Issues, Questions, and Process
- ☐ Clarifying Outcomes and Summarizing Next Steps
- ☐ Evaluation

There you go. Systematically going through this checklist will help you plan a meeting that thrives. The following chapters take a deeper dive into these meeting elements.

The Art of Centering

Begin your meeting with centering that gives people a chance to focus and gain their bearings. Meetings that begin abruptly allow no time to still emotions or collect thought and focus. People need to separate from what they have been doing. Especially when the subject matter is difficult or controversial, participants need time to breathe deeply and calm nerves. A short time for centering improves all meetings—even weekly staff meetings.

There are dozens of versions of how to open a meeting with centering. Use your favorite search engine and type "mindfulness exercises" and you will discover many choices. Here is an example of a centering exercise I have used at retreats.

> *Close your eyes. Breathe. Breathe in deeply and fill your lungs. Now breathe out. Relax. Declutter. Fill your lungs again and slowly release. As you reflect on your life, set aside the worries and stresses you bring. Breathe. Set aside those stresses. Breathe.*
>
> *Now I invite you to go to a place that is special to you. It could be a beach or a mountaintop. It could be a place at home or a place in your childhood memory. Go there now and feel the breeze on your cheek, the sound of that special place, the memories that surround it. Be there for a moment and breathe in its sacred air. Breathe a deep cleansing breath. Breathe another cleansing breath in that place.*
>
> *I invite you now to become fully present to this moment in time, where we are now. Open your eyes. Be mindful of the purpose that brought you here. Let us begin.*

In *The Pause Principle*, best-selling business author Kevin Cashman explores the ancient truth that we are our best when we slow down, take a deep breath, and pause. People come to meetings distracted by family concerns, work deadlines, a rushed meeting, phone call, or text message. Feeling rushed, pre-occupied, or stressed inhibits the ability to concentrate and be creative. Setting aside time to pause—become centered—leads to better meetings.

All religious traditions incorporate some form of the "pause principle." Buddhism teaches mindfulness. Jews, Muslims, and Christians pray. Humanists meditate. Hindus chant mantras. Most native peoples in the Americas pray and find wholeness and harmony in nature.

Albert Einstein is purported to have created the Theory of Relativity after awakening from an extended nap—a long pause. When we pause, we are not wasting time. We are respecting the precious time we have. We are more able to listen to others and ourselves with greater care and acuity.

Cushman writes:

"Pause is a universal principle inherent in living, creative systems. It is part of the order, value, and growth that arises from slowing down and stepping back. The Pause Principle is the conscious, intentional process of stepping back to lead forward and with greater authenticity, purpose, and contribution" (Kevin Cashman, The Pause Principle: Step Back to Lead Forward, *pp. 7-8).*

Pause comes in many forms: prayer, meditation, deep breathing, silence, expressing gratitude, taking a day off, hiking in nature, visualizing a place of beauty, taking a cat nap. Mindfulness helps us center on the deeper purposes of our life: to bring beauty, compassion, integrity, and humility to what we do. Creativity emerges most often after a period of doing nothing.

We help groups function better when we emanate calm even in chaos. When facilitators are centered, groups are more productive. When facilitators invite groups to pause, set aside distractions, and become centered for the work, they set the stage for a creative, productive, and healthy meeting.

The Art of Breaking Ice

Great icebreakers launch a great meeting. They dissolve barriers among strangers. Bad icebreakers freeze the ice harder and freak out introverts by demanding intimate details from strangers. At its best, a good ice breaker is a proven facilitator's strategy to make the beginning of meetings thrive.

A zillion icebreakers exist on the Internet. Written for every occasion from the first date to waiting in the line at the airport to the annual corporate retreat, they can be ridiculous and invasive:

"What fruit do you want to be when you grow up?"

"What?!"

"If you were a keyboard, what type would you be?"

"Really!?"

"What insect best resembles your personality?"

"I have no idea, but I'd like to squish the damn bug."

Cutesy icebreakers cruelly put the shy on the spot. Icebreakers that turn an extrovert into a fountain of excess may turn off the introvert's spigot.

Leader: "If you were Godzilla, what would you say to your mother?"

Extrovert: "Wow! What a great question! Mom! Blah! Blah! Blah! That was fun! "

Introvert thinking silently: "Are you kidding me? I'm out of here."

By definition, icebreakers crack the ice. People relax. The room warms up with the buzz of conversation. A good icebreaker cuts a passageway for the whole group to leave port confident, energized, and focused on the agenda at hand.

Icebreakers work best if they connect to the topic of the meeting. Icebreakers about what type of fruit you only work at a meeting of produce sellers. Icebreakers serve a dual purpose: They put people at ease and focus the mind on the topic at hand. Here are some examples:

> If your meeting is about affordable housing, ask something like, "What was the shabbiest place you ever lived and why?"

> If your summit focuses on transportation ask, "What was the most unusual trip you ever took?"

> If it is about environmental justice and climate change ask, "If you were a cheetah, where would you run and hide?"

Create a good icebreaker by writing down a list of topics included in the meeting. If you are discussing educational achievement, list "educational achievement." If designing an annual retreat celebrating the accomplishments of the last year, right down "celebrations" and "accomplishments." Next, start drafting icebreaker questions. Let your imagination roam. For the topic of educational achievement, write something that taps into memories around educational achievement:

> Describe a moment in your life when you felt proudest about your educational success.

> Name a mentor who most helped you achieve success. Describe the person and what they mean you.

> In your growing up years, what one thing that you did brings you the greatest satisfaction and sense of accomplishment now?

Choose the question that most appeals to you. Refine and edit. Show the options to a couple of colleagues and see which one they like. Then edit again. Simple always trumps complicated.

When you overhear conversations in well-designed icebreakers, you will be pleased with how folks pause, laugh and go deep easily as they engage the topic at hand.

Icebreakers don't need to be silly. They can be poignant, even tender. For example, when facilitating a meeting of biking and neighborhood advocates in Pasadena, California, I asked, "When did you first discover you could be unsafe on a bike?" People shared stories of their first fall or accident as children learning to ride. Some mentioned close brushes with clueless drivers who nearly killed them. One talked about slipping on gravel when he was six and telling his parents, "I've had a hard life. My cat ran away. My rabbit died. I fell off my bike." Another refused to answer, saying it was private. However, even in her silence, the exercise helped her and others realize the powerful emotions present that evening.

Once you have written the questions, running an icebreaker is simple. Get the group's attention using a firm voice, clinking a glass or, my favorite, ringing a chime. As a professional facilitator, I always carry a chime in my bag of tricks. Once the room quiets, give the instruction and set the group loose. Here's one final example. This was for a conference on transportation for seniors and persons with disabilities.

> "Welcome. Thanks for being here." [Announce the name of the event and its purpose.] "It's icebreaker time. Pick one person and turn to that person now. Ask him or her, 'What was it like getting to this meeting?' Take one minute to answer the question, then switch. You may begin."

There was an immediate avalanche of animated talk. Participants finished the exercise smiling and eager to hear what was next.

Icebreakers that are on-topic can be fun, expand perspectives, and maybe even touch the heart. Your icebreaker will help the group thaw and engage the event's topic. In less than five minutes, your group can be off to a great start.

Ground Rules

Ground rules, also known as behavioral covenants or behavioral guidelines, are another tool to help meetings thrive. Ground rules contain practices that embody the best values of an organization: empathy, taking responsibility, being respectful, honoring differences, being inclusive, and so on. When meeting attendees review these core values and practices at each meeting and commit to them, group behavior becomes more empathic, responsible, and appreciative of differences.

I used to think that ground rules were necessary only when a group was dysfunctional or conflicted. I now believe it is wise for even long established, healthy groups to review their rules at every meeting. Repetition reinforces desirable behavior. Repetition is good.

Ground rules are more than a list of shoulds and oughts. Scolding people is not the point. When behavioral covenants are written as practices or disciplines rather than rules, most people make a sincere effort to incorporate them into their behavior.

Note the difference between the following statements:

- We must use "I statements."

- I will take responsibility for what I think and feel by using "I statements."

The first version is preachy. It does not tell why or even how to behave. The second version contains a core value: taking responsibility. It also gives specific instructions on how to use I statements. It teaches how to embody the value of taking responsibility for one's thoughts and feelings.

The best ground rules contain both the why and what of the expected behavior. Ponder this second example:

- We will be inclusive of all voices.

- We will seek the perspectives of all by inviting each person to speak.

The difference between these two is striking. Both uphold inclusion, but only the latter embodies it practically and concretely. The second statement tells you how to be inclusive, not only that you should.

The best ground rules are crafted by engaging all participants in their creation. It is usually best for this to happen at the group's first meeting. Because the process can be laborious and protracted, I sometimes use this quicker process:

Give each member of the group five postcards. Invite them to write a practice, one to a card, that they want the organization to embody. The wording does not have to be precise at this stage. Editing will come later.

Have people form pairs and exchange ideas. Note similarities and differences. After three minutes, combine pairs into groups of four. Share key ideas, again noting similarities and differences for five minutes. After five minutes in these groups, return to a plenary format. Invite each person to share one core practice. Record the input on a flip chart or whiteboard. Invite sharing until all ideas are heard.

In just twenty minutes, everyone's ideas become part of a central list. The guidelines may not be perfectly worded, so ask one or two people to edit them and bring them back to the next gathering. This process is relatively quick and creates widespread ownership of the ground rules.

Ground rules are especially crucial in culturally diverse settings. Participants come to these meetings with different assumptions about leadership, communication, and power. Some come from cultures where people lower on the social hierarchy must be invited to speak by a person with higher authority. Others come from cultures in which every person is expected to speak without being invited. Some cultures believe silence means consent; others the opposite.

All of us have been in meetings dominated by a few people. I was a member of a citizen advisory group organized to influence transportation services for older adults and persons with disabilities. The group of thirty was recruited for diversity in race, ethnicity, gender, and national origin. Nevertheless, three white women and two white men dominated the first meeting. They were prone to interrupting when the less culturally dominant attempted to speak. The African American women, people who identified as Muslim, and the people with disabilities were largely ignored. After several meetings with similar dynamics, more than half the members dropped out. The group lost its diversity.

This group never established ground rules or a behavioral covenant. Adopting a few ground rules such as the following would have helped immensely:

- We will respect and include all voices. Meeting facilitators will invite those who have not spoken to speak. They may share or decline to speak.

- We will not interrupt. We will focus on listening as well as speaking.

The chapter on *Facilitating Culturally Diverse Meetings* describes several practices that help groups embody inclusion. For this chapter, I will focus on ground rules.

I am indebted to Eric Law and Lucky Lynch of the Kaleidoscope Institute, a faith-based, diversity and inclusion training program affiliated with the Episcopal Diocese of Los Angeles, for ways to understand and communicate inclusively in culturally diverse settings. They have taught me more than anyone how to listen, honor differences, and build inclusive organizations and communities.

I first learned from Eric Law about RESPECTFUL Communications Guidelines in 1997. I have used them, and adaptations, in many settings. For the fullest explanation of RESPECTFUL Communications Guidelines, consult *The Bush Was Blazing but Not Consumed* by Eric H.F. Law. Here is a summary:

Respectful Communication Guidelines are written in an acronym, RESPECT, making them easy to remember. I have adapted the version below from Eric Law's original version.

R = take **RESPONSIBILITY** for what you say and feel without blaming others.

E = use **EMPATHETIC** listening.

S = be **SENSITIVE** to differences in communication styles.

P = **PONDER** what you hear and feel before you speak.

E = EXAMINE your assumptions and perceptions.

C = keep **CONFIDENTIALITY.**

T = TRUST that greater truth comes through diversity.

The following are typical explanations to give for each of the letters:

R stands for taking **RESPONSIBILITY** for what you say and feel without blaming others. Use I statements such as "I think," "I feel," "I noticed," "I wonder," or "I believe." Doing so claims our experience and respects our ideas, thoughts, and feelings. Secondly, when we use I statements, we are less likely to judge or blame others for what we are feeling. For example, when someone says something that I disagree with, I might be tempted to say, "You're wrong!" A more responsible way to express my views would be, "I have a different perspective on this issue, and this is why." Some people might say, "It doesn't matter how I say it as long as I say what is on my mind!" However, in English, sentences beginning with "you" often feel judgmental and do not accept responsibility for the speaker's feelings and actions. When a person feels judged, he or she often becomes defensive and stops listening.

E stands for **EMPATHETIC** listening. Listen not just to words; listen to the whole person. Try to feel and see the world as the person who is speaking feels and sees. Of course, this is a nearly impossible task because no matter how empathetic we are toward someone, we are not that person. For example, even though I was with my wife when she gave birth, our experiences and perspectives of that day are different from each other's. This makes it reasonable to ask questions and to be patient with each other. Sometimes we need to explain what we are trying to communicate in a variety of ways so others can understand us more fully.

S stands for be **SENSITIVE** to differences in communication styles. Sensitivity to different communication styles is essential to effective, inclusive communication. For example, someone's silence in a meeting could mean agreement. Alternatively, it could mean the person disagrees, is tired, does not care, is thinking, is confused, or is waiting to be invited to speak due to personal style or cultural training. One behavior has many possible interpretations. People communicate in different styles. Therefore, do not interpret another's behavior merely based on your assumptions. Ask questions for clarification.

P stands for **PONDER** what you think and feel before you speak. Consider what you are going to say before you say it —attending to your insides before speaking communicates greater authenticity.

The second **E** stands for **EXAMINE** your assumptions and perceptions. Ask yourself, "What caused me to think or feel a certain way now? Are there personal experiences that I need to explore further before I speak?" This is another way to take responsibility for what you feel.

C stands for keep **CONFIDENTIALITY.** Keeping confidentiality differs from keeping secrets. We keep secrets to hold power or protect the interests of those who know the secret. Confidentiality upholds the well-being of the community that is being formed and the communities from which we come. Information that does not pass this test does not need to be kept confidential.

T stands for **TRUST** that greater truth comes through diversity. In a multicultural community, there will be different experiences, understandings, and opinions. There will be ambiguity. For example, different cultural groups might approach a common task in ways that are different yet appropriate to each one's culture and customs. These multiple approaches need to be honored so that, together, greater truth can be uncovered.

If you establish ground rules or covenant agreements, your group's behaviors will become more respectful, fair, and kind. The core values of your organization will move from a document into the very fabric of your group.

The Art of Flexible Roles in Meetings

In this chapter, I introduce techniques that apply to every type of meeting. People attending weekly staff meetings, longer conferences, or impromptu check-ins will all benefit. A great way to train people unfamiliar with facilitation techniques is to hand them a copy of this chapter (see my website for a free article at WWW.CIVICREINVENTIONS.COM).

Remember when you finished a meeting and were energized not only by the decisions made but by the meeting itself? Remember when you felt good about a meeting even though some issues were unresolved? Do you wonder why such meetings felt different from those that felt unproductive, frustrating, or destructive? You can increase the odds that your next meeting will be great by teaching your compatriots about roles in groups.

All of us move between different roles in our life each day. At various times, we function as a parent or child, teacher or student, supervisor, employee, friend, or partner. We step into different roles at different times in different settings.

This is the case in meetings, too. Whether in a meeting with 500 people or five, whether you are chairing the meeting or seated at the side of the table, the following roles make a difference.

Roles in groups fall into three categories: task roles, maintenance roles, and blocking roles.

Task Roles: These behaviors help a group accomplish its goals.

A. Information Seeker. Asks for facts/opinions/suggestions on the topic under discussion:

> *"What date shall we hold the event?"*
>
> *"When might we schedule a full discussion of our budget?"*
>
> *"What needs to be on the agenda at our next meeting?"*

B.   Information Giver. Offers facts/opinions/suggestions on the topic under discussion:

   "There is $300 left in the budget."

   "April second and ninth are already booked. However, the next two Mondays, April 16 and 23, are open."

C.   Clarifier. Clears up confusing statements, asks questions, checks to see that questions are answered, and keeps the discussion focused on one point at a time.

   "Let's discuss dates first. Does anyone have a suggestion?"

   "I wonder if everyone is clear on the results of our last discussion. Should we summarize them?"

D.   Summarizer. Pulls together related ideas, calls for discussion of ideas, and may write down and organize ideas.

   "It seems we're leaning towards Friday afternoon. Will that work?"

   "Is there anyone who can't make it?"

Maintenance Roles: These behaviors help people in the group get along with each other, and therefore help the group work better.

A.   Gatekeeper. Keeps communications open, encourages others to speak, gives verbal and non-verbal support to others, and suggests ways to share ideas.

   "John, you haven't spoken yet. Do you think the 22nd would work?"

   "I'm wondering if we should hear one more time from each person. Maybe some new thoughts have been generated."

B.   Harmonizer. Attempts to clear up disagreements, settles conflicts among member and reduces tensions in the group.

   "I sense some hesitation. What are the pros and cons? Let's look at the calendar again."

"I'm wondering if we are at an impasse. Would it be helpful for us to air the key items of disagreement, record them on a flip chart, and then brainstorm options for resolving them?"

C.   Encourager. Shows genuine friendliness to group members by using their names, expressing agreement, giving verbal and non-verbal support, and listening carefully.

   "Susan, I think you're right. We need more planning time."

   "José, I think we need to hear from your experience. I'd like to hear your perspective."

D.   Evaluator. Checks to see that group members are satisfied with group progress and suggests ways to keep the group moving toward its goals.

   "Is everyone OK with April 23rd[d]? If so, let's discuss what we want to do and how to keep it within budget."

   "I sense agreement. I think we've made great progress. Are we close to voting?"

The most effective groups are those in which all members use both task and maintenance roles as needed. Effective facilitators move easily between task and maintenance roles during meetings. They step into those roles not being filled by group members.

Blocking Roles: The third type of roles distracts the group from accomplishing its goals. They include dominating the group, attacking individual or group ideas, being unreasonably negative, not paying attention, and undercutting others by verbal comments or non-verbal actions. People in blocking roles are often unaware of their unhelpful behaviors and appreciate someone who graciously establishes boundaries.

The most effective way to deal with someone who is taking a blocking role is for another person to assume a task or maintenance role.

"George, I know we need to come back to that topic tonight, but I'd like us to go back to the original question of whether to paint the warehouse doors red."

"Imelda, I know it's important to review all the details of the proposal, but I sense that we're ready to vote. Could we test the group to see whether they are ready to move on and vote?"

More Tips for Facilitators

- If you know a person often functions in blocking roles, have that person sit beside you during the meeting.

- Use your body posture and a task or maintenance role to regain control of the meeting.

- Addressing people by name, summarizing what has been said, clearing up any confusion, and encouraging others is nearly always appreciated.

- Be aware of your personality strengths and weaknesses and rely on group members to fill the gaps. One of my friends who is notoriously unaware of time asks someone in the group to be his timekeeper. Another friend who is scattered and non-linear in her thinking asks the group to get her back on track if she begins to wander. I'm sometimes so task-oriented that I can seem uncaring. I often ask committees to slow me down so that everyone has time to make decisions at his or her speed.

- When orienting new members of a group or helping an on-going group develop healthy interactions, give each member a card with one role (task or maintenance) listed and described. Ask people to assume the role on their card during that meeting. Although this may feel stilted, it provides practice in a safe environment and pays long-term dividends.

- Even the most well-intentioned people slip into blocking roles on occasion. We help our groups by knowing effective, gracious ways to move them back into helpful, respectful, and productive dialogue.

The Art of Strategic Questions

Skilled facilitators know that asking the right question is the key to unlocking conversation and making meetings thrive. By listening carefully and discerning the issues a group faces, then framing the right questions, the facilitator can be the catalyst for amazing results. The right question can energize the group, focus strategy, and shift the balance toward a successful outcome. This is true for both small and large groups.

The power of questions came to the forefront during a World Café I facilitated with a congregation in Altadena, California. After a white police officer shot an African American father of seven children, this congregation decided to hold a forum. Like so many communities across America, gun violence fueled by racial distrust had visited their city. Emotions were raw, and they wanted their discussions to be safe. No open shouting matches. No diatribes or defensive speeches. They wanted a respectful dialogue on a potent subject plaguing America. They invited me to facilitate.

I recommended a World Café format (See the chapter, *Large Group Planning Methods*). Framing the right questions is essential to a World Café. After establishing ground rules and pausing for prayer, I invited people to discuss in groups of four, "How has gun violence personally affected your life?" Everyone had a story to share. Whether telling accounts of a family member, friend or work associate, the question unleashed a torrent of pain. Some form of gun violence had directly touched many.

The second round in the Café addressed the same question, again for twenty minutes. Once again, people shared personal stories. In the third round, we asked a different question: "What gives you hope?" People shared discoveries and insights. This time talk of despair and attempts to hold onto faith filled the room. I heard anger and more pain. When the group met in plenary, what the World Café movement calls a "harvest," several themes surfaced.

Some people spoke of suicide, others of domestic violence, a few talked about accidents. Most powerfully, people noticed that the emotional injuries were deep. Cultural differences aside, the most surprising insight of the group was the uniform sense of helplessness felt by police officers and lay folk, people of color and Caucasians, church members and visitors, clergy and laity. A few people said the forum, itself, gave them hope. The right question framed in the proper format had created a safety zone for honest conversation.

The best questions emerge from the facilitator listening carefully to a steering committee or planning group. An excellent first question to ask such a planning team is, "What strategic questions do you most need to ask?" or "What question, if asked, would stimulate your best thinking?"

Juanita Brown and David Isaac write that the best questions begin with a why, what, or how; rather than with who, when, or where. A great set of compelling questions can be found in their book, *The World Café*, p. 173. I have used questions like these in community meetings, governing boards, and staff meetings. Across the board, they frame discussions well and move the group forward.

Questions for Focusing Collective Action

- What question, if answered, could make the most significant difference to the future of the situation we're exploring here?

- What is important to you about this situation, and why do you care?

- What is the deeper purpose, the "big why," that is worthy of our best effort?

- What do we know so far/still need to learn about this situation?

- What are the dilemmas/opportunities in this situation?

- What assumptions do we need to test or challenge in thinking about this situation?

- What would someone who had a very different set of beliefs from us say about this situation?

Questions for Connecting Ideas and Finding Deeper Insight

- What is taking shape here?

- What do we hear underneath the variety of opinions expressed?

- What new connections are you making?

- What surprised you?

- What puzzled or challenged you?

- What question would you like to ask now?

- What is missing from the picture so far?

- Where do we need more clarity?

- What has been your primary learning or insight so far?

- What is the next level of thinking we need to address?

- If there was one thing that hasn't yet been said but is needed to reach a deeper level of understanding/clarity, what would that be?

Questions that Create Forward Movement

- What would it take to create change on this issue?

- What needs our immediate attention going forward?

- If we knew we would succeed, what bold steps might we choose?

- How can we support each other in taking the next steps?

- What unique contribution can each of us make?

- What challenges might come our way, and how might we meet them?

- What seed might we plant together today that could make the most difference to the future of (our situation)?

Great meetings deserve great questions.

- If our agency were to place advocacy for our mission at the center of our work, what would we need to do?

- If our neighborhood were to thrive, grow, and prosper, what five steps would you most prioritize?

- What question in your group or organization, if addressed, would make the most significant difference toward health and wholeness?

Archimedes said, "Give me a lever long enough and a fulcrum on which to place it, and I shall move the world." The same holds for a great question: ask the right question, and you can change the world:

- What must we do today to land a person on Mars before 2030?

- If we were courageous and bold, how might homelessness be eliminated in our city?

- If climate change demands our collective effort for the earth and our species to survive, what must we do this year, next year, and the following decade?

Liberating Structures

I recently encountered a book on facilitation and creative meeting design, *The Surprising Power of Liberating Structures: Simple Rules to Unleash a Culture of Innovation* by Henri Lipmanowicz and Keith McCandless. The book describes thirty methods to structure creative conversations on issues that matter. The authors use the term "liberating structures" to communicate that these methods liberate meetings to engage all voices and bring creativity. I describe several liberating structures elsewhere in this book (See the chapter, *Large Group Planning Methods*).

Liberating structures are designed to avoid the pitfalls of some of the most common meeting designs: lecture, presentation, and brainstorming, to name a few. Such designs are often dominated by a few people, typically leading to boredom and low participation. Liberating structures, on the other hand, engage all participants, generate creativity, and, when used systemically, transform the culture of an organization toward greater inclusion.

The structures described in the book by Lipmanowicz and McCandless are ways to launch what the authors call "a culture of innovation." Each is designed to include all voices. They liberate participants into more productive meetings.

One of my favorites from Lipmanowicz and McCandless is called *1-2-4-All*. The facilitator poses a question on an issue of concern to the group. For example, "How might we be the safest workplace in our city in the coming year?" Individuals take one minute to list key ideas on a piece of paper. Then, in pairs, they quickly share their ideas (two minutes). They notice similarities and patterns and strengthen their combined ideas. Next, pairs combine into groups of four to share, compare, and coalesce ideas in four minutes. The final stage is a plenary session: the "All" in *1-2-4-All*. Each group of four shares one key idea with the whole group, popcorn style, avoiding duplication. The results are recorded for all to see on large post-it notes or a whiteboard.

In fifteen to twenty minutes, *1-2-4-All* harvests the collective wisdom of a group with everyone's participation. In a short time, *1-2-4-All* generates energy, excitement, and engagement. Unlike groups in which someone drones on and on or a hearing in which people give two-minute speeches, the results from *1-2-4-All* are wildly democratic. No one remains silent unless they ask to pass. Groups are set free to create and innovate. It's cool.

I used *1-2-4-All* in the second of two transportation summits to craft ideas for strengthening the way seniors and persons with disabilities secure transportation. The first of these summits lasted five hours. We completed two World Café rounds, plus announcements, breaks, and lunch. It was wildly successful, generated significant results and positive feedback. The second summit needed to pack in many of the same items, as well as a 30-minute resource fair—but in three hours instead of five.

Because each World Café round takes ninety minutes, we needed a different design that would fit the reduced timeframe. So, we used one round of *1-2-4-All* followed by one round of a World Café. We budgeted twenty minutes for *1-2-4-All* and ninety minutes for the World Café. Both methods engaged participants in widening circles of conversation. Each method created energy. Each mined the collective imagination of participants like gold from ore. It was, again, a successful summit.

The *1-2-4-All* question was merely, "What challenges do I face when searching for transportation?" Eighty voices engaged at once. Each person was seen and heard. The room was abuzz like bees excited about their queen. At the plenary harvest, the collective experience popped from the crowd. In the space of twenty minutes, every participant had contributed his or her thoughts. Each heard the ideas of the others. Inviting the group to participate in a *One-Two-Four-All* design got the summit off to an incredible start.

A second example of a liberating structure is the conversation circle. We see conversation circles in many places: tribal councils, coffee klatches, Bible studies, basketball breaks, and football huddles. All use the geometry of the circle. Circles do not need a head facilitator. Small circles are self-regulating. They need no experts, leaders, or priests on high. One facilitator is sufficient to set up the room, get out of the way, and help record results.

The list of liberating structures is ever expanding. I encourage you to grab a copy of the book and visit the website at www.LIBERATINGSTRUCTURES.COM

Large Group Planning Methods

The last thirty years have seen remarkable innovation in the art and science of large group planning. Inspired by community organizing, the women's movement, and contemporary pedagogical theory, planning methods such as Appreciative Inquiry, World Café, Open Space Technology, and others have revolutionized the way organizations plan and engage stakeholders in strategic conversation.

These meeting technologies share approaches. All share the insight that conversation is at the heart of how humans build knowledge, imagine our future, and gain commitment. Through language, we look beyond the landscape of now and imagine new horizons of tomorrow. Talk is our work. Whether we talk informally in the kitchen, on the patio, at the water cooler; or more formally in meetings, conferences, and summits, conversation is central to what we do. We plant seeds, imagine dreams, and affirm collective action. Talk is essential.

These methods are "appreciative." That is, they build on strengths rather than needs, deficits, or problems. Switching from deficiencies to strengths releases imagination. New solutions emerge on the foundation of what people do best in an organization, rather than on fixing what is wrong.

These methods rely on creative questions to release conversation and creativity. Crafting the right question is central to gaining more in-depth insight, inspiring forward movement, and bringing focus and energy. All combine small and large group conversations. Small groups create intimacy and invite all to participate. Large, plenary sessions ensure the meeting results are distilled and shared.

The methods affirm that system-wide change is possible when all stakeholders engage in strategic talk. They reject the tired belief that only elites should participate in strategy. Radically democratic practices replace top-down, hierarchical assumptions about organizational change.

Large group methods vary in the length of time they require. World Cafés can take as little as ninety minutes. Open Space Technology events may last one, two, or three days. Some designs take 20 minutes or less.

The facilitator's role varies in these methods. Some require facilitators to be hands-off while others need a more active presence. Some need a degree of structure to guide the conversation. Others are quite loose and unstructured. The best combine structure and freedom of expression.

The outcomes of each large group method also differ. Future Search is best for achieving a shared vision of the future. Open Space and World Café focus participants on core issues and questions driving the organization. They can result in the formation of detailed plans if given sufficient time. The outcomes for Appreciative Inquiry are many and focus on process as much as results. Appreciative Inquiry releases a group's imagination and strengthens organizational vitality. It clarifies and enhances a sense of shared values. Organizations using Appreciative Inquiry consistently report a change in corporate culture from hierarchical decision-making to democratic, egalitarian practices.

New large group planning methods emerge all the time. Each technique has a library of resources written to guide facilitators, coaches, and consultants. I have listed my favorite titles in *Future Reading*. The following pages describe a few methods I find most useful. Visit my website for articles on many of the practices at www.civicreinventions.com.

Appreciative Inquiry

Appreciative Inquiry is a fundamental shift in how we address organizational change. The conventional way to facilitate change is to identify a problem, analyze it, and invent a solution. The focus is on problems to solve. We focus on the broken parts and try to fix them. These methods inadvertently amplify problems by putting a spotlight on the negatives.

Appreciative Inquiry emerged in the 1980s as an alternative approach. Community organizers have known for decades that coalitions and advocacy are most effective when building on the strengths and assets in a neighborhood, not its deficiencies. David Cooperrider and his colleagues at Case Western University developed Appreciative Inquiry to use this approach and focus on what works in an organization. It is a strengths-based approach.

Appreciative Inquiry has several principles. The first is that every group, business, and organization has something that works, something good. Even the most tired organizations have a kernel of success upon which to build.

The second principle is that what we focus on creates our reality. If we focus on problems, our reality will be about problems that need fixing in another person or an organization. If we focus on strengths, we will see a person's gifts and the positive aspects of our business and organization.

The third principle is that the act of asking questions shapes the way organizations think. Questions mired in problems generate organizations that get mired in fixing problems. Questions that invite creative exploration help organizations embrace the future and innovation.

Appreciative Inquiry looks at the history of a group or organization and invites attendees to notice key moments of success: times of vibrancy, creativity, and energy. Here is an example of Appreciative Inquiry in an annual strategy retreat:

> Assemble a group for the annual strategy retreat of a business association. The retreat attendees include staff, the board of directors, and a handful of volunteers.
>
> After the preliminaries (the welcome, an icebreaker, and the like), begin the heart of the meeting with something like the following: "Today we are going to discuss these questions: 'What did we do well in the past year? What was it that gave us our greatest success?'"
>
> After participants pick their jaws up off the floor from the shock of being asked to focus on strengths rather than problems, they begin to stream answers.
>
> "It was our block party."
>
> "It was the long table event."
>
> "It was when we invited the whole community into a celebration of good food, great music, and fun."
>
> "I liked when we invited new board members, and they brought such great ideas."
>
> "No doubt, the hiring of our new executive director."

In the next stage, the facilitator invites participants to explore another appreciative question. It might be, "In the coming year, how shall we build on our success?" or "Given our successes last year, what bold steps shall we take in the year ahead?"

Again, ideas pour forth.

"We need another block party, only let's shut down three blocks instead of one and invite the entire city."

"We could invite six restaurants to cater the event, instead of one. The variety will increase attendance."

"Maybe we could get corporate sponsors and discount the tickets."

"Maybe we could invite a jazz band. I know a superb group."

Notice the focus on strengths, not problems. The facilitator might have asked, "What shall we do about the problem of some businesses not supporting our work?" That question is draining, devoid of energy, and dripping with fatigue. An Appreciative Inquiry question would, on the other hand, be something such as, "What makes our association attractive to new businesses and old? How might we strengthen our welcome and engagement for all businesses in our downtown?"

Appreciative Inquiry is immensely adaptable. Appreciative Inquiry can be used in all types of settings from corporate boardrooms to neighborhood groups, and informal conversations. For example, when I see a staff member in the morning, I often ask an appreciative question such as "What good is happening in your life these days?" They tend to share stories of hobbies, children, or a new relationship. It is amazing how asking about good things and strengths turns the conversation into an energized moment.

Examples of Appreciative Inquiry questions abound. Here are a few:

- What has gone well in your day? (Great for getting teenagers to talk.)

- What one thing are you most excited about in the next year?

- What's good in your organization?

- How might we build on our improved safety record in the coming years?

- What organizations and businesses in your neighborhood bring strength to your coalition's work?

- What has been most helpful to your work in the past year? How might we build on it?

Organizations have more ability to travel into the future if they carry with them the best of the past. If a bookstore has a history of holding political forums that pack in crowds, there is a pretty good chance that political forums should be a part of the coming year's schedule. If a congregation has found energy and joy in serving meals to the homeless, then its future will likely be built around food and serving the poor. The past is prologue. Our organizations thrive when we bring forward the best of our history.

The *Further Reading* section in the back of this book has resources on Appreciative Inquiry. The most comprehensive is *Appreciative Inquiry Handbook: For Leaders of Change* by David Cooperrider, Diana Whitney, and Jacqueline M. Stavros. Order a copy soon.

The World Café

The World Café is another way to structure democratic conversations around questions that matter. It works in groups numbering from twelve to the thousands. World Café is an approach to strategic collaboration that engages all voices and energizes groups. Most importantly, it is democratic. When used as a core element in a strategic planning process, it results in system-wide ownership.

A World Café begins with participants gathering in groups of four or five around small, round café tables. Tables are covered to resemble a French café, frequently with red-checked tablecloths. Flower vases, a candle, and a cup of brightly colored markers adorn the tables. A few sheets of large flipchart paper are placed on the tables for people to record ideas, doodle, and draw. (Groups may need to set aside some of the table decorations to write on the flipchart paper.)

Participants explore "questions that matter." Questions are shaped specially for the challenges before the group. They must be written carefully to stimulate greater thinking, release imagination, and create commitment. Asking the right question makes a difference in how the group discovers knowledge and commits to action. See the chapter on *The Art of Strategic Questions* for examples.

A typical World Café has three rounds of twenty minutes, followed by a thirty-minute plenary called the "harvest." Everyone, except the person hosting each table, moves to a different group following each round. The host shares highlights from the previous conversations with the newbies at his or her table, inviting cross-pollination of ideas and insights. As conversations connect, they spark discoveries and expand collective knowledge. After ninety minutes of table conversation, participants share their insights, learnings, and opportunities for action in a whole group harvest.

I have hosted dozens of World Cafés: at a homeless shelter engaging staff, neighbors, and homeless guests regarding how to ensure the shelter's success; with a residents' association developing key public policy strategies, and with faith-based groups imagining their future. I am always amazed by the energy, imagination, and collective intelligence that emerges in the harvest.

Like all the methods described in this chapter, World Café is grounded in the hypothesis that ordinary people have wisdom. Every group, organization, coalition, and business has the chops and creativity to imagine their future through strategic conversation. They can confront the most difficult challenges and the most potent issues of our time.

Six principles guide World Cafes. They are outlined in the book *The World Café: Shaping Our Futures through Conversations That Matter* by Juanita Brown and David Isaacs. I have adapted the principles described below from their book.

1. **Set the Context** – Attend to why you are bringing people together and what you want to achieve. Context includes who should attend, what questions will generate the most creativity, and how the design of the harvest.

2. **Create Hospitable Space** – Meeting spaces make a difference. You want one that feels safe and inviting. When people feel comfortable, they think creatively and listen better.

Make your invitation warm and welcoming. Create a welcoming atmosphere.

3. **Explore Questions that Matter** – Craft questions relevant to the real-life concerns of the group. Powerful questions attract collective energy, insight, wisdom, and action. The most powerful questions are open-ended, invite curiosity, and emerge from the lives of the people involved.

4. **Encourage Everyone's Contribution** – Welcoming every participant's contribution is central to a World Café. Recognize that everyone has ideas and thoughts to share. Nonetheless, some people prefer only to listen. The World Café method provides a structure for both sharing and listening.

5. **Connect Diverse Perspectives** – New ideas and discoveries develop as participants move between tables and meet new people. New perspectives, insights, and recognition emerge.

6. **Listen Together for Patterns and Insights** – Listening well determines the success of a World Café. By listening and paying attention to themes, patterns, and insights, the whole group discovers wisdom. People see new connections, shared themes, and insights.

7. **Share Collective Discoveries** – Conversations at one table connect with conversations at other tables. The harvest makes these connections visible to the whole group. Encourage a few minutes of silent reflection on the patterns, themes, and deeper questions experienced in the three rounds of small group conversations. Then, invite the larger group to share common insights and discoveries. Capture the harvest by working with notes and a graphic recorder.

The World Café method has successfully engaged all kinds of groups across the world. Used by women's health collectives in Sub-Saharan Africa seeking improved health outcomes for women and children and by Fortune 500 corporations imagining better ways to improve safety, the method is versatile and effective.

For more information about the World Café movement, check out the website at WWW.THEWORLDCAFE.COM and order the book, *The World Café: Shaping Our Futures through Conversations That Matter*, by Juanita Brown and David Isaacs.

Open Space Technology

Open Space Technology was developed in 1985 by Harrison Owen to address complex issues. Open Space is a democratic process for groups as small as five and as large as 2000. It engages all voices of an organization in one to three days. One day results in intense, worthwhile engagement. Two days produce a report of the proceedings. Three days generate an action plan.

Open Space's strength is full enrollment in both process and results. It will not work in organizations that assume elites at the top of the food chain know far more than the peasants. Senior management will feel too threatened, while subordinates will not speak their minds.

As in a World Café, meeting room set up for an Open Space event is atypical. Upon arriving, participants see a space with one, two, or three large circles of chairs. Various signs are on the walls; including a schedule, the principles of Open Space, and a strategic question to be addressed. The most disconcerting feature is the lack of an agenda. The agenda will develop later.

The first essential ingredient in an Open Space event is that participants fashion the agenda during the event. Every agenda item in the participants' minds related to the strategic question is fair game: the more ideas and greater diversity, the better. The second essential ingredient is that everyone needs to care. People who don't care should stay home. Everyone should have a stake in the future of the group. Participants need passion and a willingness to take responsibility. Because participants shape the agenda, energy and engagement replace low ownership.

An Open Space event begins with a simple invitation. While most meeting invitations include an agenda, Open Space Technology does not. Open Space invitations convey the usual items about location, times, and food arrangements. As far as the meeting contents go, they say something like the following: "We will discuss the question [fill in with an innovative, challenging question]. Every issue important to you and the [organization] will be explored. We will hear all the voices. We will be energized. We will set priorities. We will issue a full report. If you bring passion to [organization] and a profound sense of responsibility, we need you to attend. Everyone else stays home."

The room layout must permit one, two or three concentric circles of chairs (depending on the number of participants), plus breakout space for small groups. The circle must be large and open—hence the name "Open Space." Breakout spaces can be in the same room, nearby in separate rooms or some combination. The definition of a room is flexible. Breakout spaces could be outside in a park, alongside a swimming pool in a hotel, or a coffee bar. You will need five or six breakout spaces for every one hundred participants. A long blank wall adjacent to the large circle suitable for posting signs and agendas completes the picture. A bank of computers and printers can be made available at one end of the room if you decide to record proceedings and generate reports in real time.

Meeting planners need to figure out meals, refreshments, and breaks. Supplies include nametags, masking or artist's tape, brightly colored markers, flip charts, and lots of large post-it notes. If the group is large, a microphone and speakers will help. No matter what size the group, you will need microphones if some people use hearing loop devices or have limited hearing.

Prepare and post signs. These provide the minimal structure of Open Space Technology. They include the following, described in greater detail below.

- Theme, Behavior, and Expectations
- Daily Schedule and Space/Time Matrix for the Wall
- Report Production

One sign gives the theme of the event. Carefully frame the purpose of the event in a question with as few words as possible. It must reflect a central issue or aspiration of the group. Generic questions will not work. The question must be specific and evoke deep passion and thought.

- How shall we embrace technological change with seniors?
- How shall we become the safest work site in our company?
- How shall we eliminate homelessness in three years?

- How shall we erase the tragedy of gun violence from our nation?

Questions must be big and bold, and your group must not already know the answer. Easy questions with easy answers are out. You want evocative, exciting, open-ended questions that elicit new thought and intense conversation.

You need four more signs. One sign lists the following four guidelines:

- Whoever comes is the right people.
- Whatever happens, is the only thing that could happen.
- Whenever it starts is the right time.
- When it's over, it's over.

The second sign says:

- Be Prepared to Be Surprised.

The third sign says:

- The Law of Two Feet—If during the gathering, people discover they are neither learning nor contributing, they must use their feet and go to a more productive place.

The fourth sign is a large sheet of paper with a time/space matrix. The time/space matrix specifies times across the top row. The left column lists meeting locations.

The blank wall is used to post topics that will comprise the agenda as the meeting develops. The meeting starts with nothing on the wall but a barebones meeting schedule. The schedule provides starting and ending times, lunch, and the times for ninety-minute sessions spread over one, two, or three days.

As the facilitator, you create a welcoming, open space. You should arrive early, make sure everything is arranged: supplies available, signs posted, and refreshments set out. Then relax. There should be no rushing around when participants arrive.

For detailed instructions for room setup and meeting preparations, consult chapters 5 and 6 of Harrison Owens book, *Open Space Technology: A User's Guide.*

Here's how it works for a multi-day, large group.

(Scale your event to size as necessary. Use an outside facilitator or someone from your organization.)

The circle or circles are set. The space in the middle is open, save for a collection of brightly colored markers, tape, and lots of sheets of small flip chart paper. The task for the first ninety minutes, no more, is to set the stage, focus the group, state the theme, and describe the process.

Open Space Technology meetings launch with a brief welcome. "Good morning, I'm glad you are here. You've all read the invitation and know why we are here." Then the leader restates the question that will drive the Open Space meeting. Something like, "We are here to explore the question, 'How might we make a difference in stopping gun violence?'" or "Our driving question today is 'How shall we strengthen our commitment to equity and inclusion?'"

If there is an outside facilitator for the event, introduce her or him next. Be brief. "It's my pleasure to welcome Mark Smutny, our facilitator. He is an author, professional facilitator, owner of Civic Reinventions, and today's host. Let's welcome Mark."

The facilitator takes the floor. "Good morning. I'm Mark. Welcome to our Open Space. Today we are in for an exciting, productive day. Let's begin." Keep it brief. No flourishes or speeches. No icebreakers or the like.

After the welcome, invite the group to look around and see who is present. As the facilitator, your calm presence is essential for this step. Encouraging people to look at each other in these opening moments is a way to create a safe, inviting space. Quiet respect is the goal.

Next, restate the central question of the meeting in a way that brings focus. "We are here today, tomorrow, and the next day to generate a detailed report highlighting the steps and resources needed to change our neighborhood from a high crime, low investment disaster into an economically-thriving and culturally-diverse engine of commerce, culture, and community. By closing time on Wednesday, we will have produced a detailed work plan."

Avoid long speeches and cute icebreakers. Skip last year's strategic planning results. Forget naming the longest-serving employees and giving them plaques and gift cards. Cut to the chase.

Review the signs on the walls. Read each one out loud. Stay upbeat. Convey a can-do attitude and a spirit of optimism.

Next, describe the process. Mention that Open Space Technology has been around since the 1980s and has been used all over the world. Paint a picture of an Open Space event. "Imagine two hundred people gathered in one room, self-organizing a conference with forty breakout groups spread over two days, with a complete, one hundred page report detailing goals and objectives for the next two years. Amazing!"

Then say, "This is how it works." Quote from Harrison Owen's *Open Space Technology: A User's Guide,*

> *You may be wondering how we are going to do all this. It's quite simple. In just a little while, I am going to ask each of you who cares—and nobody has to—to identify some issue or opportunity related to our theme for which you have a genuine passion and for which you will take real responsibility. Don't just consider good ideas that somebody else might do or be interested in. Think of powerful ideas that will grab you to the point that you will take personal responsibility to make sure that something gets done.*
>
> *If nothing occurs to you, that is okay, and if you have more than one issue or opportunity, that is fine too. Once you have your issue or opportunity in mind, come out into the center of the circle, grab a piece of paper and a marker. If you have more than one issue, take several pieces of paper. Write down a short title and sign your name. Then stand up in front of the group and say, "My issue is . . . and my name is. . . ." After you have announced your theme, take your piece of paper and tape it up on the blank wall (pg 88).*

Underscore two points: First, to come forward with an idea requires passion. Secondly, coming forward means you are willing to take responsibility. These twin needs enable people to go forward and then facilitate the next step.

As a skilled facilitator, you know some anxiety is good. Anxiety can improve learning and increase engagement. Capture that anxiety by saying something such as, "Never been in a meeting where the agenda is a blank wall? Guess what? In one hour, you're all going to be saying, 'How will we possibly get through all this with only three days?'"

Explain that taking responsibility means topic proposers must name a time and place to meet and then convene the session. They must also be willing to record the proceedings on a computer. Each convener places a post-it on the time/space matrix, indicating the theme, time, and location for the meetup.

The final step before releasing people to the meetups is to review the four principles and one law. These outline the way things work in Open Space.

The first is *"Whoever comes are the right people."* In other words, if two people show up with a similar passion, that's enough.

The second principle is *"Whatever happens is the only thing that could happen."* Real learning and growth occur when we are open to surprises. Greater truth and insights emerge.

The third principle is *"Whenever it starts is the right time."* When conversations get rolling, some people jump immediately to the question at hand. Others want to chat informally. Some want to share pictures of their dog, cat or child. Creativity in groups emerges through trust and trust develops by giving people time to warm up. My advice for the "do everything on time" participants is to remind them to breathe deeply and go with the flow.

The final principle is *"When it's over, it's over."* If your group fashions its ideas in thirty minutes when the schedule says you are allotted ninety, quit when you are finished. Go somewhere else. Open Space Technology encourages flexibility. Do not waste time in a meeting that is finished by trying to figure out something else to discuss.

The one law states, *"If during the gathering, people discover they are neither learning nor contributing, they must use their feet and go to a more productive place."* This law is a great leveler: If one person is in love with his or her voice and dominates air time, other people have permission to leave. They walk away. There is nothing like walking away to convey that a different, more respectful behavior is required. So, if the discussion becomes boring or you discover your most profound passion lies in another group, take a walk.

As the facilitator, you need to remind people of one last item: *"Be Prepared to Be Surprised."* The wonder of Open Space Technology, like all whole group planning methods, is that the process of creative conversations uncovers new knowledge. Greater wisdom emerges. Reminding participants to anticipate surprise prepares them for wonder, and yet-to-be imagined results.

Now, launch. Press the button and let the rocket take off. Say something like, "Now, I invite everyone who has a deep passion for an idea and is willing to take responsibility for convening a group to come forward. Grab a post-it and a marker. Record your idea. Say, 'My issue is. . . . My name is . . . .' Then place your post-it on the space/time matrix and rejoin the group."

A ten-minute circus breaks out with people posting issues. The group will likely generate more topics than you have slots available. Group similar items together. Once the space/time matrix is finished, invite participants to look at it, ponder their interests, and work out what group they will attend for the first round. Hit a bell and announce the convening of the first session.

The rest of the day organizes itself. Each break-out space needs flipchart paper and markers. At the end of each ninety-minute session, ring a bell to let people know the session is finished. Collect the note-filled sheets. Put them on the blank wall. Encourage conveners to type their flipchart results.

Tell people when each session starts and remind them about the *Law of Two Feet*. With these parameters, the event will run itself. Whether you have a one-, two-, or three-day event, make sure each day has thirty to forty minutes near the end for the whole group to reflect on the day. The focus should not be on the substance of the issues but the process. Ask, "What went well today? What do you suggest we improve?"

Once people get rolling, Open Space is easy to facilitate. I guarantee that your organization will discover great energy and focus on an issue central to your group.

Appreciative Inquiry, World Café, and Open Space Technology are but a few of the large group planning methods that now breed like flies. Future Search, Process Mapping, and Planning Charrettes are a few of the other most commonly used methods. Each seeks in various ways to engage all parties and embrace diverse perspectives.

Room Layout

Room layout makes or breaks a meeting. We most commonly attend meetings of six to twenty-five people with tables and chairs arranged in a rectangle, U-shape, or square. This arrangement works well with a skilled facilitator and cooperative attendees. The chairperson or moderator sits at the head table, while the board or committee members sit along the sides. This arrangement focusses power in the chairperson. Such an arrangement can be helpful to the chairperson if a member tries to undercut her authority, as well as helping her see everyone at the table. However, full inclusion depends on a skilled moderator who ensures everyone is invited to speak. Group members can help a moderator ensure full inclusion by assuming the roles described in the chapter, *The Art of Flexible Roles in Groups*.

If possible, form a small oval or circle instead of a rectangle. Because oval and round tables have no corners into which people can disappear, the facilitator and attendees are likely to notice everyone. Making this change may cause greater participation. People who are usually quiet will be more likely to speak. Make sure the circle or oval does not have too much interior space so you can foster relative intimacy rather than distance.

If your group numbers more than twelve, experiment with a non-traditional setup where people sit at several small round tables, four to a table. The facilitator can sit at one of the tables. Design the agenda to have at least one topic discussed in small groups. Then design a whole group process for hearing each table's key ideas. The level of participation will skyrocket.

To engender discussion, encourage creativity, and garner insights in a large meeting, consider one of the two room layouts below.

1. Scatter small, round café tables around the room with four or five chairs at each. This format invites conversation. Proximity to each other makes it easier for participants to intervene if one person becomes verbose. Café

tables encourage listening and remaining mentally present in the meeting. When people sit at small café tables, they easily introduce one another and engage in animated conversation on the topic for the day. Thousands of people in a vast conference hall can experience intimacy and full engagement when meeting around café tables.

2. Large round tables that seat six or eight people create a different dynamic. Conversations will tend to be sideways in twos and threes. This can be effective if you want groups of two or three to discuss a topic, then join the larger group at the table for a second level conversation.

Even the best room arrangements can miss the mark if the meeting format undercuts inclusion and conversation, as happened in a meeting I recently attended. A medium-sized nonprofit had spent more than a year creating a meticulously-written plan of equity, inclusion, and diversity for every department. The leadership made the plan's rollout the focus of an annual all-hands retreat. They filled the meeting room with enough café tables to seat roughly two-hundred people in groups of four or five. I was hopeful.

Unfortunately, the meeting fell as short of its goal as a first-grader trying to make a field goal from the 50-yard line. After distributing the report, someone stood at the front of the room and gave a lengthy explanation. The group went silent except for the random shuffling of paper and feet. Next came a hard-to-hear, rapid-fire, extensive presentation on the impact of racism. The presenter's Powerpoint text was too small to read from the tables. When the participants could neither hear nor see the presentation, they lost interest and began texting and reading their smartphones.

The café tables embodied the values in the report—one might say the table was set for egalitarian, energized conversations. However, the meeting design undercut the small groups seated at the tables. The agency fumbled a great opportunity to model its commitment to inclusion.

If the event had included a large group method such as a ninety-minute World Café, the outcomes could have been astounding. In a World Café, they might have asked, "How might your work or department implement the values of equity, inclusion, and diversity with bold, courageous steps?" Then the room would have erupted in a crescendo of creativity. Participants would have felt included, valued and heard. They would have left the retreat energized and hopeful. Their collective wisdom would have nurtured growth and further development across the agency. The room layout, meeting format, and final results would have had internal, reinforcing consistency.

Go ahead and mix it up. Break out of the typical presentation and lecture room design. Use pairs, circles, ovals, small and large tables. If a presentation is required in a large gathering, put the speaker in the center of the group, surrounded by widening semi-circles of chairs. Each of these room layouts will change the group dynamic for the better. Trust me.

Facilitating Culturally Diverse Meetings

The journey toward inclusion begins with mindfulness of unconscious cultural attitudes and assumptions. Because many of the most common meeting designs inhibit inclusion, inclusive facilitation techniques and meeting design are the next steps.

Typically, most meetings are dominated by a handful of people, with the remainder staying silent. Silence can mean agreement, disagreement, fear, or even anger. Silence might say people have checked out mentally and are thinking about their to-do list or where to go on vacation. Silence can also mean that the people not speaking come from a culture in which it is considered rude to talk without having been invited to do so.

Some cultures assume that everyone in a group will be assertive and speak up, although that rarely happens. Shy people are often excluded simply because more dominant speakers eat up all the air time. Other cultures expect only leaders to speak. Peoples of that culture will not speak unless first invited by a person in authority. Still other cultures have discovered that passing a talking stick, speaking staff, or similar device invites full participation.

I've experienced countless meetings in which white Americans are in meetings with people from nations and cultures that have different expectations about how people should communicate. The white Americans dominate the meeting because their culture rewards verbal assertiveness. Meanwhile, people from many of the other cultures expect an invitation to speak. Without an invitation, they stay silent. Then, after the meeting, the white Americans wonder why the others did not talk. They are frustrated with the difference between their expectations and the behavior of the people from other cultures.

In the meantime, the people from cultures who expect to be invited before speaking perceive the white Americans as rude. They complain (quietly) that the loud Americans talk without being asked. They observe that the most aggressive Americans jockey for attention. What unacceptable, obnoxious behavior those white Americans exhibit!

Building inclusive conversations when participants come from diverse cultures with different assumptions about leadership and speaking in public requires recognizing these differences and adapting for them. Skilled facilitators notice who has not spoken and invite them to speak. When only a few people dominate a meeting, the facilitator extends an invitation for others to speak. The facilitator can ask the following:

- "We have heard from some of you; now I'd like to hear from those who have not spoken. Who hasn't spoken?"

- "I'd like to hear another perspective. Who hasn't had a chance to speak?"

- "Now that we've heard from some, would anyone who hasn't yet spoken like to strengthen what has been said?"

These questions empower the reticent to speak.

Another way to include people from a variety of cultural backgrounds is with small group discussions of four or five people. Groups of this size can be inherently inclusive. Many contemporary large group discussion methods including Appreciative Inquiry, World Café, and Open Space Technology are designed to be inclusive of all voices. They combine small groups and plenary sessions to benefit from the inclusive nature of small group discussions.

Strategies for including persons with disabilities in meetings are essential for them to be equitable and just. I have dedicated a chapter to discussing accommodations for persons with disabilities. It's a big topic. See the chapter, *The Art of Including Persons with Disabilities.*

Ground rules or behavioral covenants frequently affirm the importance of including all. The chapter on *The Art of Ground Rules* includes a set of ground rules designed to build inclusive meetings.

Some indigenous peoples of the Pacific Northwest use talking sticks to build inclusive conversations. In tribal meetings, the Tsimshian use beautifully carved lengths of wood to command authority and invite others to speak. The person who holds the talking stick is granted authority to speak. That person speaks, then offers the stick to another, who now has the power to offer his or her thoughts. After each person is finished speaking, the stick is handed over to another. The process is repeated until all present have had an opportunity to speak. Those with years of wisdom speak, as do the young. The talking stick can be an effective means to ensure the voices of all are heard in many groups numbering less than twenty.

Objects other than a stick can serve the same purpose as a talking stick: a stone, paperweight, candle, or goblet. I bought a twelve-inch wooden rod at Home Depot, painted it barn red, and carry it in my facilitator's tool kit to use as a talking stick. A talking stick builds democratic participation. It helps ensure that all voices are heard: old, young, men, women, girls, and boys.

One of the most powerful tools I have encountered for building inclusive conversations is *"Mutual Invitation."* Developed by Eric Law, an American Episcopal priest born in Hong Kong, reared in New York City, and now living in Los Angeles (three international cities), Mutual Invitation recognizes that communication styles and patterns vary across cultures.

Mutual Invitation accommodates these differences. It empowers the shy and constrains the verbose. It recognizes that everyone has unique insights from life experience and culture. Mutual Invitation encourages democratic participation, regardless of cultural background or power differential. It is respectful, empowers those who are reserved and cultivates deeper listening

In Mutual Invitation, the facilitator speaks first, then invites another person to speak. The facilitator usually chooses someone not seated directly beside himself or herself. Going around a circle inhibits listening because the person who expects to speak next is thinking about what to say instead of listening to what is being said. Short-circuiting that cycle helps the group listen to one another instead of merely preparing their responses.

Once a person is invited to speak, that person can choose to speak, to pass or to pass for the moment. No matter which of these options is chosen, she or he invites another person to speak when finished. In the end, the group leader offers anyone who passed for the moment another opportunity to speak. The process continues until everyone who wishes to speak has done so.

Eric Law emphasizes the importance of the language of invitation. Inviting a person allows each person to participate in the power of facilitation. If you invite me to speak next, you are exercising power to choose me. I have the power to respond or not. I also have the power to extend an invitation to the next person. The act of inviting is a subtle, important type of power. See Eric H.F. Law. *The Wolf Shall Dwell with the Lamb*. pp. 79-88. WWW.KSCOPEINSTITUTE.ORG/MUTUAL-INVITATION

Facilitating Multilingual Meetings

In global corporations, local neighborhoods, nonprofits, and public sector organizations, meetings that accommodate multiple languages are increasingly in demand. Immigration, ease of travel, and economic globalization call for skilled multilingual facilitators. With the techniques outlined in this chapter, you can make your next meeting a mosaic of different languages and cultures.

Facilitating multilingual meetings is challenging and complicated, even difficult. Some organizations have the resources to hire interpreters, translators and translating equipment. Other organizations with fewer resources can still hold meetings with up to three languages. This chapter addresses how to make bi-lingual and tri-lingual meetings inclusive and effective, no matter the size of your organization or group.

When you are going to mix two or more languages in a small group, try to include some bi-lingual people. They are an important resource because they can translate for the group. If you have a tri-lingual group, people who speak all three languages are an amazing asset. Identify these people ahead of time and brief them on the topic and format for the meeting.

When planning and facilitating multilingual events, facilitators need to speak all the languages represented or invite someone who is multilingual to translate and co-facilitate. Because plans made by one language tradition and imposed on others will not be received well, all language groups must be represented on the planning team. Equitable meetings begin with equitable planning.

Write invitations in all languages expected at the upcoming event. One invitation might include all the languages, or each group can receive an invitation in its language. Agendas, emails, flyers, hand-outs, and PowerPoint presentations must also be translated into multiple languages. Send these materials to interpreters and translators well in advance. Interpreters and translators should be alerted to difficult words or concepts. Brevity is essential when more than one language is involved because each statement needs repeating in every language. Yes, these details are challenging. But they are worth the effort.

At the event, the welcome should be spoken in all languages represented. All handouts and presentations should be multilingual, although if the group is overwhelmingly of one language, not everything after the welcome needs to be spoken in all languages. The smaller language groups will still need bi-lingual interpreters and translators. Contemporaneous translating in which interpreters speak into a radio headset and participants listen on earpieces is an alternative under these circumstances. This type of device can easily be rented. Some municipalities, schools, and congregations own such systems and make them available to outside groups.

Ground rules are especially important when facilitating meetings in which multiple languages are present. The RESPECTFUL Communications Guidelines outlined in *The Art of Ground Rules* are specifically designed for multicultural and multilingual settings. They encourage empathy, recognize differences in communication styles across cultures, and prescribe steps to help make meetings welcoming and inclusive. Translate the RESPECT Guidelines into the languages likely to be spoken at your event.

Mutual Invitation or a talking stick can be helpful in multilingual groups numbering less than twelve. Talking sticks take too long if the group is larger than that. If possible, break the group into smaller circles in which you can use talking sticks. This helps you benefit from the rich diversity of attendees.

World Café and other whole group planning methods described in this book work well with multilingual groups. They include small groups of four or five and plenary sessions in which the insights and ideas of all are reported and recorded. When using these methods, cluster people in language-specific groups. For example, in a tri-lingual gathering, have tables specifically for English speakers, Spanish speakers, and Mandarin speakers.

Dividing participants into language-specific small groups accomplishes several goals. First, conversation flows more easily without having to wait for a translation. Second, it strengthens trust among participants. People better understand each other's nuances and inflections when they share a common language. Some cultures, particularly new immigrant communities, feel safer when conversing with people who speak their language. They often feel intimidated in groups dominated by participants of the majority culture—even when the majority culture folks do not intend to be intimidating. Safety generates trust. Third, language-specific groups have greater confidence in speaking when it is time to report in the plenary sessions.

You might think of language-specific groups as caucuses. Caucuses are where people discuss needs, plan strategies, and gain confidence. When caucuses present their demands and ideas in or negotiate with, a larger group, the time spent in small groups pays off. People representing less-dominant cultures speak more forthrightly than they would have otherwise and linguistic groups with less power feel more confident.

A common mistake of well-meaning planners is to have all cultures and languages together in a Kumbaya moment. I've been there, done that. The reason this rarely works is that different cultures and language groups have different amounts of power. In the United States, for example, English speaking groups have more power than Spanish speakers, Korean speakers, or almost any other linguistic tradition. While there are times when it is important to mix people in a wonderful tapestry of colors and backgrounds, it needs to be done with care and intentionality.

The problem is power. Power differentials block full participation unless intentionally addressed in the group process and structure. The well-meaning dominant group will wonder why the other cultures are quiet. They do not realize that some cultures will not address conflicts directly. These cultures articulate disagreements in oblique ways, if at all. For them, preserving outward harmony is more important than speaking or reaching agreement. Remember, silence can have many meanings, from total agreement to complete opposition.

Designing meetings with language caucuses helps break down these power differentials. Later, when caucuses join the plenary session in which all languages are represented, speakers from less dominant groups are more assertive and less likely to suppress their ideas and thoughts. Also, because comments are made on behalf of the group, no one loses face. Caucuses build confidence and make for more inclusive outcomes.

Multilingual meetings are challenging and exciting. They are not easy to facilitate. Skilled multilingual facilitators can seem as rare as a kimchi taco truck in Southern Italy. There may not be much market for those tacos, but there is a growing market for skilled facilitators of multilingual meetings.

Including Persons with Disabilities

The Americans with Disabilities Act became law in 1990. Since then, awareness of how to include persons with disabilities has skyrocketed. Nonetheless, meetings frequently have little or no accommodations for persons with disabilities. Even groups committed to inclusiveness too frequently exclude. Listening, building awareness, and training can reverse these exclusive practices.

In this chapter, I include some recommendations for meetings in which persons with disabilities are recognized as equals and their gifts honored. I encourage everyone who values inclusion to read further in this area than this short chapter permits.

The need for skilled facilitators able to work with a range of persons with disabilities and to craft meeting designs accordingly cannot be overestimated. The number of persons who need accommodation is staggering. According to the U.S. Census, 57.6 million Americans reported having a disability in 2010. Over 20 million of these either "have trouble" seeing even when wearing glasses or contact lenses, are blind, or unable to see at all. Thirty million have a hearing loss. One in eight people in the United States aged twelve years or older have hearing loss in both ears. Approximately 8 million Americans have some mobility impairment that necessitates the use of adaptive equipment such as a cane, crutches, walker, wheelchair, or scooter. Sixty million Americans nationwide have learning and attention issues. Millions more struggle with autoimmune disorders, cancer, diabetes, service-connected disabilities, or cardiovascular and respiratory challenges. Temporary disabilities from falls, accidents, and broken bones number in the millions as well. With the number of aging baby boomers growing, these statistics will climb. As the truism says, "All of us will eventually have a disability."

Preparing for meetings with persons who have disabilities begins long before the meeting. Considerations include meeting location, parking, entrances, exits, the meeting room or rooms, and the location of restrooms. People with mobility disabilities want to know if there are safe and convenient drop-off areas, sidewalk cutouts, and safe and wide pathways to the meeting rooms. Like everyone else, they want to know where to find the food, beverages, and restrooms; and where to register attendance. Some will want to sign up for the next gig, buy a book, or know where to find the petition to lobby elected officials.

The planning team and facilitators begin by listening. Who will the attendees be and what advice do they have about accessibility? Persons with disabilities are the experts, along with their companions and advocates. Listening to their needs begins the inclusive planning process.

The meeting planners need to address a variety of questions. Will the event need to be on one level? Will captioning be required? Will a signer be needed? Will a companion dog attend? Will a full transcript of the proceedings be helpful? Will invitations need to be in Braille or is large print sufficient? Do aisles and table layout need to accommodate mobility devices such as wheelchairs, scooters, and walkers? Are assistive listening devices needed? What type of furniture and layout facilitates full participation? Asking these questions up-front goes a long way toward inclusion and making meetings accessible. Empathy, decency, and fairness require that they are asked.

Meeting planners may need to arrange for recording the proceedings in real-time for persons who are deaf, hearing impaired, or who need a readable record to trigger their memory. Graphic recorders can be an excellent choice for visualizing and summarizing meetings. Graphic recordings benefit the visually dominant, persons who cannot hear, and those who are hearing impaired.

People with mobility needs require the meeting room to be configured for wheelchairs and other devices. Expand narrow aisles and clear obstacles. Braille handouts and large print versions may be required. Guide dogs need to be accommodated. Signers and caption writers may need to be recruited.

One way to communicate that your group values inclusion is for the invitation to contain details about the meeting's accessibility. Receiving an invitation and noticing that the event will accommodate one's needs builds trust. People feel welcomed and honored. They are more likely to attend and will engage more fully in the meeting.

If possible, send out agendas, PowerPoint files, charts, and other handouts in advance. When agendas and supporting materials are received ahead of time, participants can more easily prepare for the topics. This improves meeting flow. Participants need to calculate the time required to get to the event and their return, so include starting and ending times in communications to help everyone plan accessible transportation.

Greeters are an excellent way to welcome everyone when they arrive at the meeting location. For those who are blind, greeters are essential. They can describe the pathway to the meeting or escort the person whose sight is impaired to the first stop.

If a registration table is needed for signing in and receiving handouts, make sure that people with mobility disabilities can approach the table. The same goes for refreshments. Make sure the tablecloths are short—no long hanging frills and frippery. Be ready with kind people to help fill plates and glasses for those who need help. If needed, help bring full dishes and liquid refreshments back to a person's table.

If there is a podium where a speaker or facilitator stands or sits, make sure it is adjustable. When possible, a better selection is a table with chairs and microphones. If there are interpreters, translators and signers, make sure they can be seen. For the leader or facilitator, provide a small table with a glass of water and a place for notes. If a raised platform from which people will speak is not accessible, do not use it. Bring a table down in the crowd—it will enable all to participate. As a side benefit, having people sit at a table on the same level creates intimacy and warmth.

For those who are blind, facilitators should briefly describe the room layout and location of restrooms and refreshments. Describe the location of tables, chairs, and podium. Remove clutter and keep aisles open. When meetings begin, invite participants to share their name when they speak. This allows the blind to know who is in the room and who is talking.

If the meeting includes audiovisuals with projected slides, summaries of discussions on whiteboards, or flip charts, the facilitator should describe what she or he sees.

When contracting with interpreters, translators, captioners, and graphic recorders, planning teams should be aware that it may take weeks to line up professionals whose services are in high demand. Begin planning early. Before the event, facilitators should dedicate time to talking with interpreters, real-time captioners, and graphic recorders to describe meeting expectations. Provide handouts, agendas, and background material to help these professionals plan.

On the day of the meeting and well before the session begins, have the facilitation team review the set-up. Make sure that seating, lighting, and equipment are in place. Review the table setup and other fixtures to make sure no obstacles exist in aisles and between tables. Test assistive listening devices. Make sure that interpreters are adjacent to speakers and facilitators and that sight lines are clear.

Making meetings accessible and accommodating persons with disabilities are not lofty goals. They make practical business sense. The amazing variety of life experience and the stamina and courage it takes to navigate life as a person with disabilities means that all of us should cherish their contributions.

Facilitators, planners, and consultants who seek to learn from and comply with the ADA requirements can find a wealth of resources and training online. Articles, checklists, and webinars abound. For designing accessible meetings see WWW.ADAHOSPITALITY.ORG/TOPIC/PLANNING-ACCESSIBLE-MEETINGS. For a complete list of ways to accommodate persons with disabilities, visit ADATA.ORG, the website of the Americans with Disabilities Act National Network and its ten regional centers. Other nations have similar resources.

Interest-Based, Principled Negotiating

Leaders are frequently called upon to mediate conflict and negotiate solutions. While conflict can be an opportunity for creativity and growth, toxic conflict inhibits progress and makes life miserable.

Some groups spend years dealing with conflict in unproductive ways. Dysfunctional behavior seems to be in their DNA. Nonetheless, such behavior can be unlearned and replaced with healthy habits. Teaching a group to negotiate well can be an essential strategy for improving organizational health.

Negotiating well is a learned skill. Whether you are negotiating a union contract, crafting a budget, facilitating a strategic plan, bringing culturally diverse parties together around a common mission, or merely resolving a conflict among staff members, being able to negotiate well helps you navigate the shoals of conflict and sail with the wind at your back.

Thirty years ago, Roger Fisher and William Ury of the Harvard Negotiating Project introduced millions of people to the art of principled negotiation in their bestseller, *Getting to Yes without Giving In*. Their alternative to positional bargaining has a proven record in labor/management negotiations, international treaties, divorce settlements, and many other types of conflict.

Most of us are accustomed to positional bargaining. It is the traditional, most well-known method of negotiating in which one side prepares a series of demands and the other side responds. For instance, a union might make a series of demands on wages, benefits, and work environment. These demands are backed by a constituency who wants the negotiators to drive a hard bargain. After the union representatives present their demands to management, management prepares a response. Management comes back with strength and offers a counterproposal that is typically less than the union wants.

The union representatives walk away, consult with their members, and perhaps threaten a strike. They return with a counter-proposal. Both sides see the other as adversaries and try to squeeze as many concessions from them as possible. Parties who give in are considered weak and soft. Those who hold firm are considered strong. At the end of the negotiation, both sides usually remain unsatisfied, already planning for their next conflict.

Principled negotiation is a welcome alternative to positional bargaining. Fisher and Ury list four steps to the method.

1. Separate the people from the problem.

Whether coming from a position of strength or weakness, emotions can get in the way. People's egos get entangled with the objective merits of a problem. In principled negotiating, people's feelings are disentangled from the substance of the conflict. The structure of the process helps to contain emotions and set them aside. Emotional containment permits the problem to be attacked, not each other.

2. Focus on interests, not positions.

A negotiating position often obscures what a party wants. Underlying every position is an interest, sometimes many interests. Interests deal with people's underlying motives, needs, desires, concerns, and fears. An interest is what causes you to decide on a position—reconciling interests rather than positions works because most interests can be satisfied in a variety of ways. When you look behind opposed positions for the motivating interests, you can often find alternative positions that will meet some of the interests of both parties.

For example, in the negotiation of a commercial lease between a landowner and a tenant, the landowner may have several interests: the desire to make a reasonable profit, keeping other tenants happy, having a well-cared for facility, reducing costs associated with tenant improvements, attractive signage, and low costs for utilities, insurance, maintenance, and managers. The future tenant may want clean floors and restrooms, low utility costs, lights that work, a responsive and responsible manager, rental rates that are low and stable, and attractive signage that markets the business and helps customers find the offices.

The interests of the tenant to have clean floors and restrooms can be met in several ways. The tenant could clean, have the landowner clean, or contract with a third party. The landowner's interests to have a happy, satisfied tenant can be met by keeping the restrooms clean and the floors sparkling by using his or her elbow grease, hiring a cleaning company, or reducing the rent and having the tenant assume the responsibility.

Note that behind the opposed positions lie shared and compatible interests, as well as conflicting ones. Shared interests and differing interests provide the building blocks for a wise and lasting negotiation.

Inquire into why the parties have made their choices. If you are trying to change their minds, try to figure out where their minds are. Each side has multiple interests. List and explain them. Declare interests boldly but be soft on the people. Rarely does each side have identical interests. Identify and name the problem areas.

In our example, both parties hold the following interests in common:

- A desire for happy, satisfied tenants.
- A desire for clean floors, restrooms, and a well-maintained facility.
- Predictable rent.
- Long-term tenancy.
- Keeping other tenants happy.
- Low tenant improvement costs.
- Low utility costs.
- Lights that work.
- Low insurance costs.
- Attractive signs.
- A responsive and responsible manager.

The following interests are not common to both parties:

- Making a profit.
- Rental rates stay low for a long time.

As a negotiator, invite the parties to list their interests. Display them on a whiteboard, flip chart, or electronic display. Ask the parties to circle the interests held in common and check the ones not shared. Engage the group. This step is critical. Engaging the parties in identifying interests motivates them to move to the next step and generates ownership when the time for solving problems arrives.

3. Generate a variety of possibilities before deciding what to do.

Invent options for mutual gain. Brainstorm. List. Avoid premature judgment. Avoid searching for a single answer. Banish the assumption that the pie is fixed in size or shrinking. Do not think that "solving their problem is their problem." Engage everyone in generating options. Invite the group to note the most promising ideas. Strengthen those. Tweak them. Name whether underlying interests are likely to be met. Point out that there may be more than one best solution.

In our example of a shared interest in having clean restrooms, floors, and a well-maintained facility; participants might generate the following:

- The tenant cleans.
- The landowner's son cleans.
- The landowner hires a cleaning company.
- The tenant hires a cleaning company.
- The tenant, who is a nonprofit organization, hires and supervises homeless people to clean the facility and, in so doing, creates new jobs.
- The tenant takes responsibility for cleaning only the kitchenette. The landowner takes responsibility for the restrooms and floors.

Notice that one common interest generates multiple solutions. Positional bargaining often leads to parties getting stuck. In principled negotiating, people are freed to be imaginative. Principled negotiating engenders collective imagination.

4. Insist that the result is based on objective criteria.

The final step is to identify objective criteria to evaluate options. Optimistic talk about win-win solutions does not conceal the reality that often interests conflict. Differences cannot be swept under the rug for long.

Positional bargainers attempt to deal with differences by talking about what they are and are not willing to accept. Hard bargainers give bottom lines and arbitrary deadlines. They stake out extreme positions well beyond what the other party wants in the hope that the other party will be "weak" and cave. Soft bargainers make generous offers seeking to preserve peace and friendship. In both scenarios, the negotiation deteriorates into a contest between wills. Rarely is the negotiation efficient or amicable.

The solution is to negotiate on a basis that is independent of the will of either side—that is, by using objective criteria. The selected solution should be based on principle, not pressure or whim that fails to stand the test of time.

Objective criteria may be based on either fair standards or fair procedures. Fair standards are often grounded in precedent, efficiency, costs, moral standards, equal treatment, tradition, or reciprocity. Through the process of negotiation, conflicted parties agree which objective standards they will use to weigh the appropriateness of the best solutions.

Alternatively, a fair procedures approach may be used to develop objective criteria. Fair procedures might include the decision to let a more objective group decide, such as a board of directors, an administrative judge, or a panel of arbitrators.

To determine which standards to use for measuring a successful negotiation, frame each issue as a joint search for objective criteria. The process is intuitive. Do not yield to pressure, only to principle. Ask "What's your theory?" "On what value do you base this?" Ask questions such as, "Is this the precedent you want to set?" "Is this the standard of fairness that you want to utilize for similar situations?"

Back to our example. As the facilitator, ask the parties, "What standard will help us move this negotiation forward?"

The participants might respond:

> "The landowner should make a fair profit."
>
> "The landowner should not make an excessive profit."
>
> "We all agree some profit is appropriate."

The facilitator asks, "What objective criterion would help us set the rate of profit? What ideas do you have?"

Possible responses:

> "The rate should be indexed to the cost of living, plus 3%."
>
> "The rate should reflect the average of what other commercial landlords are receiving. The local board of realtors has that information. We could use that rate as a standard."

Identifying the appropriate objective standard reduces the role of emotions in the negotiation. It engages the creativity and imagination of the parties again.

Positional bargaining rarely advances our interests when we bring deep hopes, fears, and passions to a negotiation. With positional bargaining, a problematic negotiation frequently sets the stage for future conflict. When using interest-based, principled negotiation, not only can practical outcomes be achieved, the results can be healing. Mutual problem-solving can replace protracted conflict.

Principled negotiating is not always successful. Sometimes parties' interests do not intersect. However, whether negotiating international treaties between global powers or a spat among neighbors on where to locate a new park, interest-based, principled negotiating can be remarkably effective. Conflict is inevitable, but it need not be toxic, debilitating, or persistent.

Facilitating Difficult Meetings

Everyone has attended difficult meetings. Personalities clash. Interests differ. Emotional issues get in the way. Weak leadership and toxic personalities block progress. The purpose of the meeting is as clear as mud. Quick naps and yawns spread like dandelion seeds in a summer breeze. With meetings like these, we are tempted to run for the meadow and never come back.

Troubled meetings are made more difficult by the polarization of our times. Seemingly insurmountable divisions abound. From the halls of our schools to the halls of Congress, we hear about the loss of respect, the decline of decency, and how people seem unable to find unity of purpose across political party lines. We are a divided people.

Societal issues divide us: immigration and border security, gun violence and the freedom to own weapons, healthcare and taxes, racial injustice and white supremacy. The politics of race, gender, class, and religion tear our social fabric. Religious groups split over any number of social issues from the role of women, to abortion, to gay rights. As Americans, we recall few times in our nation's history when we were more divided.

Local communities experience similar division. Teachers and school boards fight over salaries and benefits. Police departments and citizens are at loggerheads over shootings and race. City councils and citizens fight over scarce resources. Both near and far, we are a divided people.

Nevertheless, I believe that respectful dialogue is possible. Respectful conversations across divisions can bring healing and hope. With the right techniques, tools, and a spirit of care, our conversations need not be fraught with mistrust and fear. Groups, organizations, and governments can move beyond a cycle of division and despair.

This chapter introduces resources to help you facilitate difficult meetings. I hope that you will feel equipped the next time you tackle a tough meeting. As always, practice makes perfect. Read the book, then do the work. We have a great need for skilled facilitators in our troubled times.

Facilitating difficult meetings begins with the facilitator. When facing a divided crowd, a poised facilitator can inspire participants to rise to a higher level of mutual respect and practical problem-solving. Facilitators who are emotionally mature and spiritually-centered are more able to facilitate with skill and forbearance.

Forbearance and patience are practices described in the chapter, *The Art of Emotional Resilience,* in which I underscore the importance of mindfulness and emotional forbearance. Building personal resilience and a spiritual center long before a meeting begins is essential. When we are centered, we are better able to facilitate a troubled group. People sense confidence and personal strength in leaders. Groups calm down and are more able to focus. Our frontal cortex overrides our fearful reptilian brain. Spiritually-centered leaders build trust so a pathway through conflict can be found.

On the other hand, when nervousness exudes from the pores of a leader, the group worries and stays tense. Collective anxiety breeds collective distrust. With anxious leaders, conflicted groups are more likely to fight and fight dirty.

Exuding confidence and calm is not always easy. We operate out of internalized beliefs about conflict, usually unconscious, that shape the way we respond to conflict. These life commandments form in childhood. They emerge as emotional responses to conflict within the family system and the broader culture. Life commandments may include messages such as:

Avoid conflict at all costs.

Never reveal your feelings.

Be stoic in all settings.

Don't fight.

Be nice.

Fight hard, or you'll be seen as weak.

We can work through this. Hang in there.

Conflict can be creative.

Conflict is constant.

Stay quiet, and you might escape.

Lance the boil. Ease the tension. Make things return to a more relaxed state.

Keep making jokes. With jokes, you can avoid getting hurt.

Grab all the attention. Make them focus on you.

Work things out behind closed doors. Don't fight in front of the children.

Everyone has life commandments. These internalized messages shape our behavior with results ranging from good to disastrous. If you are one of the few whose family treated conflict as an opportunity for creativity and mutual respect, you are truly blessed. Your gut tells you "I can do this." The rest of us mere mortals had imperfect families.

My family of origin taught me both helpful and unhelpful life commandments. Reared with an older sibling who regularly picked fights, I learned how to fight back—verbally. I honed a caustic, quick, verbal knife. I fought with words to survive my brother's aggression. Sometimes it worked. Sometimes not. Sometimes I could get him to back off. Sometimes I resorted to fists. The memories are painful.

In high school, a friend pointed out that my sarcasm and quick retorts hurt others beyond my brother. I did not want to be someone who hurts others that way. I began to change. I learned to contain my mouth (usually), and cut out sarcasm (mostly). I tried not to retaliate when under threat (often). It has taken years of reflection. Therapy helped, as have prayer, lots of practice, and reminders from my wife. Growth and change do happen.

My family of origin taught me some positive life commandments about conflict as well. I learned it is possible to forgive and that I can be forgiven. I learned that despite the tension, things could get better. I learned you could move through conflict and get to the other side. These positive beliefs became a part of me as well. I have developed a positive belief that I can draw on to check my anxiety about conflict. I optimistically believe that by working hard to understand one another, conflict can be good, even helpful.

Containing my life commandment about fighting back has made me a better facilitator. In difficult meetings, I try to contain the urge to be aggressively verbal. Like adding a tag to the end of a recording, I often cap my aggressive life commandment with an alternative. This one says, "Don't get defensive. Don't be baited. Facilitate. Help the meeting go well. Use your conflict management and listening skills. Command authority. Help them fight fairly. You and they will be fine."

These alternative messages do not eliminate my urge to lance conflicted meetings with a sharply honed barb. They control it and manage it. By managing my childhood response with the wisdom of a seasoned adult, I am more able to run a meeting, even a toxic one, with poise. It also helps if I heed my mother's advice: get eight hours of sleep, eat well, exercise, and count to ten before opening my mouth and saying something I will regret.

When we become mindful of our life commandments, we can choose how to act. For example, mindfulness allows our frontal cortex to choose forbearance instead of fear. Taking slow breaths to calm our heart rate calms our fight or flee instinct as well. When I facilitate a difficult meeting, and my gut starts to wrench, I take a few deep breaths, face forward, and facilitate with wisdom. You can, too.

Your life commandments about conflict differ from mine. One person might believe that conflict is the worst thing imaginable, while another thinks moving through conflict is the path to new life. One person might believe consulting village elders is the best way to resolve conflict, while another cannot imagine speaking of the conflict beyond the nuclear family. Some respond to conflict by bullying. Some react in ways personal to their deep trauma and abuse. As a facilitator, you need to be mindful of your deeply embedded commandments and, if these are unhealthy for the current context, cap them with a healthier alternative.

Once you have your head on straight and you can contain whatever fears you may have about conflict, the next step is to launch the meeting. Begin the session with authority—command people's attention. Never begin meetings with an excuse.

Do not say:

"I'm sorry. I might not be good at this."

"There may be another person who could do a better job than I, but I'm the one you've got, so let's get started."

Or the all too common, "Excuse me. I'm sorry for interrupting your conversations. Could we begin?"

Aargh! No! No! No! Making excuses straight out of the gate is a terrible way to begin (a habit more often found in women than men according to my non-scientific observation). When you start with excuses, you undercut your authority and communicate the opposite of the steady hand, optimism, and gentle authority the conflicted group needs.

So, stop the excuses. Sound confident. Fake a sense of authority if you don't feel it. Say boldly, "I need your attention. It's time to begin. Let's get started." When in doubt, be bold. The group needs you to project confidence that you can steer them through choppy water.

The next step in working with divided groups is to craft ground rules. Developing ground rules together builds ownership and gives you a sense of how the group will function. (See the chapter, *The Art of Ground Rules.*)

I always like to seed the discussion of ground rules with a few of my favorites. The first one I usually suggest is, "I will take responsibility for what I feel and believe by using I statements."

I offer a humorous example: When I tell my wife, "You burned my scrambled eggs. You're never careful," she tends to get ticked off and defensive. On the other hand, if I say, "I notice my scrambled eggs have an off taste. I'm struggling to eat them," she sighs and laughs. Then she says, "Yeah, the puppy peed on the floor again, and I forgot to pay attention to the eggs. Well, I usually forget to pay attention to the eggs. Sorry." Then she suggests I cook the eggs the next time.

Ground rules during conflicted meetings may include the following:

- One person speaks at a time.

- We will use I statements to express what we think and feel.

- We will listen to one another and empathize with the other person's point of view.

- We will ponder our thoughts and feelings before we speak.

- We will keep confidences unless the group agrees to share selected information beyond the group.

- We will attack issues, not people.

- We will trust that we discover greater truth by hearing multiple viewpoints.

The next step is to get the group to relax and become centered. Mindfulness exercises help. Consider deep breathing, meditation, or stretching. Even just a few arm stretches can help the group release some of the poison infecting the room.

Now you are ready to address the core conflicts and issues that trouble the group. Multiple meeting designs can help. Here are a few.

If the conflict is in a group with a long history together and there are difficulties with the direction of the group, the *Constructing an Organization Timeline* exercise may help.

If the conflict centers on a troubled negotiation between parties, *Principled Negotiation* can help.

If the group numbers twelve or more, a World Café design or similar large group technology (see *Large Group Planning Methods)* can be helpful. In these designs, participants engage in conversational circles numbering four or five to a table to address a question or issue. The inherent intimacy of a small table generates better listening. Carefully compose the question that each table will address.

If you want respectful dialogue on a difficult topic in a community meeting, the best strategy is to break the large group into smaller, café type conversations. The hearing format typically used by governments—in which people speak at a microphone for two or three minutes—is perhaps the most frustrating and pointless meeting design imaginable. The problem with hearings is they are not conversational and rarely interactive. Their sole benefit is to ventilate. Occasionally, they inform. Thousands of hearings litter the political landscape. Ineffective meeting design destroys opportunities for real learning.

Venting is not dialogue. The receivers of the venom grow defensive. Cutting off two-minute mini-speeches when the speaker is in agony over the death of a loved one is cruel and ultimately pointless. The alternative is to structure conversational dialogue. Conversation circles, a World Café, or meeting in small groups of four or five for multiple rounds followed by a plenary session works much better.

Here's how an effective community dialogue works.

Select a meeting venue that is warm and inviting. Send invitations that state precisely what you will and will not do. For example:

> You are invited to a community dialogue on race and police shootings on Sunday evening from 6:00 - 8:00 p.m. at the Freedom Community Center. We will discuss the recent police shooting and the role of race. We invite faith groups, social clubs, neighborhood residents, the police, and elected officials to attend. We will engage in respectful dialogue. We will not attack one another. We will produce a list of next steps to achieve better communication and understanding and move our community toward greater racial justice and respect for all persons.

Use all forms of communicating the invitation: email, snail mail, posters, public service announcements, social media, announcements at faith and community groups, and word-of-mouth.

When the time for the meeting comes, do not arrange the room in a hearing style format with rows of chairs facing a panel of experts or officials. Eradicate that format from your repertoire. Use café tables with four or five chairs at each. Decorate the tables with a tablecloth or multicultural table runner and a small vase of flowers. Place markers and flip chart paper on each table. Or seat people in small circles without tables. If need be, use rectangular tables but set up only two chairs on each side. (See the chapter, *Room Layout.*)

Expect people to be surprised by the room set-up when they arrive. They will expect row after row of chairs, with a podium and microphone in the front of the room. Instead, they will see small tables and chairs that look inviting and hospitable. They will be invited to sit wherever they choose. There will be no particular table for elites. The mayor will sit side-by-side with the hurting mom; a police officer will sit across from the local priest, rabbi or imam; and the unemployed renter will sit next to the business owner. Embrace diversity. Diversity and equality are your friends.

As the facilitator, begin the meeting with a warm, confident welcome. Re-state the meeting's purpose and use an icebreaker to ease the group's tension. For example, "In pairs, for two minutes each, share your name, where you were born, and why you chose to show up for this meeting."

Establish ground rules. I suggest using the RESPECTFUL Communication Guidelines covered in the chapter, *The Art of Ground Rules*.

In small groups of four, discuss the following questions for twenty minutes: "Why did you decide to come to the meeting? What life experience led you here?" People are to share and record their key thoughts on the flip chart paper at their table. A detailed description of World Café design elements is in the chapter, *Large Group Planning Methods*.

After twenty minutes, mix it up. One person stays behind at each table while the others travel to new configurations at other tables. For twenty minutes, the groups discuss the same question or a second question that invites them to go deeper. For example, a question for the second round might be, "How has gun violence personally affected my life?" Be prepared for lots of emotion and compelling stories. With easy access to firearms in the U.S., stories of violence and suicide will pour out. Be prepared.

Repeat the process with a third twenty-minute round. Address the question, "What bold steps should we embrace going forward?" At the end of round three, convene a plenary session—a harvest. Report out the highlights of what was discussed in the three rounds.

There are many ways for a facilitator to structure the plenary session. You can invite each table to report in popcorn style. You can place all the key ideas on giant post-it notes. (I love to use 11" x 11" post-it notes.) You can ask a small group to sort all the notes, grouping them by category and calling out the highlights. You can get creative. The point of the plenary session, or harvest, is to capture the collective experience and insights of the whole group.

Invite the entire group to reflect on their experience of the event. Ask the questions, "What did you notice? What do you wonder?" Be prepared for more anger and hurt, and discoveries of commonality across divisions. For example, be prepared for people of all races, backgrounds, and jobs to share stories of gun violence that have injured or destroyed lives.

Conclude the meeting with reflections on how the meeting went, then focus on the next steps. Summarizing next steps communicates action and hope. This format works with all kinds of issues. From immigration to neighborhood growth, café conversations beat public hearings, hands down.

Now and then, you might encounter groups so toxic that even the most skilled facilitator finds them a challenge. Meetings in which someone's goal is to destroy others do happen. If you discover you are facilitating a group where some of the attendees are over-the-top furious and unable to calm down, do not proceed with the meeting. Abandon your agenda.

For example, if you discover in the middle of crafting ground rules that a person repeatedly interrupts and attempts to derail the process, tell the group that you are unwilling to proceed. Declare a ten-minute break and say, "When I return in ten minutes, I will see if this group wants to proceed with the agenda of establishing ground rules. If not, I will leave and find something else to do with my time." Leave the room and find someplace to relax. Take deep, cleansing breaths. Collect your thoughts. Return after ten minutes. Invite the group to decide whether the meeting will continue by focusing on ground rules. If they say "Yes," proceed. If the same dysfunctional behavior breaks out, collect your things and walk away. Find something else to do. Take a walk. Drink a favorite beverage. Watch a movie.

Throughout conflicted meetings, the facilitator will benefit from utilizing the listening skills of fogging and negative inquiry covered in the chapter on *The Art of Listening Skills.* These skills help facilitators de-escalate aggressive behavior.

Difficult meetings are legion. I hope that the suggestions above help you facilitate with confidence and calm. Good luck. Peace be with you in your difficult meetings.

Facilitating Strategic Plans

A common management tool requiring skilled facilitation is the strategic plan. Well-facilitated strategic plans can help organizations set priorities and focus energy, and help stakeholders work toward common goals. They strengthen how businesses and nonprofit organizations respond to changing environments. They do not predict the future, but they help you prepare for it. They are especially helpful when leadership has changed or a shift in the market stresses the business or organization. The need to embrace new technology, reach new customers, or re-energize a group's mission are a few reasons why launching a strategic planning process makes sense. Strategic plans provide structured conversation to respond intelligently to these threats and opportunities.

The best strategic plans focus organizational priorities and enroll all stakeholders in the results. Both the plan and enrollment are crucial. A strategic plan with system-wide buy-in will produce practical, measurable, time-specific results. With regular evaluation, you will know when you are successful. Poorly designed strategic plans are ignored and make fantastic fire starters. Good ones can be awesome.

Strategic plans are hard work. They demand time and resources. Undertaking them can stress an already burdened organization. Nonetheless, they produce results. When designed and facilitated well, they create multiple settings in which creative conversation about the future occurs. People generate the best ideas for embracing the future with imagination and creativity. Teamwork builds, and a strong sense of community breaks forth. Ownership grows as stakeholders redefine mission, vision, and the values that will guide their behavior.

In strategic conversations, people decide what is central to the organization. They make decisions on how to deploy resources of time and talent. Detailed work plans create a roadmap for success to increase profits for businesses and further mission for nonprofits. When the essential step of evaluation is built in, strategic plans guide organizational behavior and drive adaptive change.

An insider to your organization or business can facilitate your strategic plan. A board member, CEO, or a strategy officer can certainly do the job. However, hiring a professional facilitator to guide strategic planning can be a wise step. An outside consultant frees leadership to participate fully and brings objectivity. The workload for an insider can be overwhelming because facilitating and writing a strategic plan takes resources and time.

If your organization has never undertaken a strategic plan, several excellent books are available to guide you. Buy one tailored to the organization you serve. Books written for businesses are slightly different from those for the nonprofit and public sectors. These books will make you more knowledgeable for your own work and when hiring a facilitator.

Undertake strategic plans every three years. The pace of change is so rapid that five- and ten-year plans become irrelevant.

All strategic plans share common steps.

1) Organize a planning committee that represents diverse interests within your organization. Include the top executive, board chair, a few board members, and senior managers. Consider including a few line employees and lower managers. By recruiting employees lower on the food chain, you signal that everyone is important in the planning process.

2) Use a skilled facilitator, usually someone outside of your organization who can lend objectivity and free all stakeholders to participate without distraction. Having the CEO, executive director, or board chair serve as facilitator is usually a mistake. No matter how talented, she or he cannot be objective. A neutral facilitator is especially helpful when dealing with contentious issues. The consultant listens carefully to your organization's unique needs and strategic challenges. She or he facilitates planning meetings, focus groups, and the planning retreat; crafts questionnaires; sets schedules; and drafts the plan. The consultant should be disciplined, deliver results on time, and have high personal integrity.

3) Conduct an environmental scan that assesses your organization and the environment in which it operates. The scan is both an internal audit and a market study. *SWAT Analysis* is the most commonly used environmental scan. Others include *Porters' Five Forces* and the *Pestle Analysis*. Regardless of the type, they accomplish the same goal. They provide data on organizational health, strengths, weaknesses, and external market conditions—both threats and opportunities. Also, collect data through in-person interviews, written and online questionnaires, and focus groups.

4) Agree on three or four strategic goals. Strategic plans that emphasize more than this number become diffuse and hard to remember. Set aside the other goals for your next plan.

5) Hold a strategic planning retreat that engages all stakeholders. Gather the collective intelligence and ideas of everyone who has a stake in your organization. During the retreat, you will create or revise your mission, vision, and values statements. You will discuss priority areas and decide on key objectives. You will use a tool such as SMART (Specific, Measurable, Achievable, Relevant, and Time-bound) to make a detailed plan.

The retreat must be inclusive to maximize buy-in. Include all levels of employees from line workers to middle managers and senior executives. Invite funders or investors. If a nonprofit, include neighbors, political officials, and advocates. The plan will be a waste of time with less than full participation. Rulers can no longer say, "Jump!" and expect the peasants to ask, "How high?" Involve everyone. The payoff will be a strategic plan that lives and breathes across your organization. Shareholders will be impressed, and funders will fall in love. Employees will parade the plan at every meeting. Water will turn into wine—almost.

6) Draft the written plan. The consultant typically drafts the report in dialogue with the planning committee. Edit it without mercy. Chop out jargon. Reduce the plan to simple, direct sentences that convey action, vibrancy, and hope.

7) Vet the plan with the board of directors and senior management. Hold focus groups with direct service employees. Encourage corrections, and strengthen the plan until it is perfect.

8) Adopt the plan. Usually, a Board of Directors or similar group approves the final version.

9) Promote the plan. Gussy it up with cool graphics and make it a thing of beauty. Print it on glossy paper. Saturate your organization with copies. Post it on your website and blog about it.

10) Most importantly, read it. Read it in new employee orientations. Refer to it in meetings. Place it in gathering places. If you make it central to your organization's life every employee, funder, supporter, and volunteer will know its content. You will be impressed by how much everyone affiliated with your organization is on board, knows your strategic priorities and the work plan that makes it happen.

11) Conduct regular evaluations. Schedule system-wide meetings exclusively for reviewing the plan one year after its adoption. Begin with the board of directors, then expand to other stakeholder groups. Review the plan carefully. Celebrate progress. Make course corrections. Invite improvements. Two years out, review again. In three years, initiate a new strategic planning process. With change rushing by like whitewater, five-year strategic plans are like a canoe without a paddle.

The value of strategic planning lies in both the process of arriving at the plan and the written plan itself. The planning process engages people in system-wide conversations about priorities and objectives. It creates multiple opportunities for imagining the future. The plan sets direction and guides performance for the years that follow. With the right design, the right facilitator, and multiple occasions for input, buy-in can be nearly universal. Buy-in triggers better performance. Your organization will thrive.

Facilitating Systemic, Organizational Change

Facilitators and executive coaches are frequently called upon to mentor leaders in making systemic change in their organizations. Whether the goal is implementing new technologies, acquiring a new company, restructuring the organization, breaking down silos, or changing the organizational culture; effective change requires specialized leadership.

Making a systemic change in an organization is difficult. Common reasons include the absence of urgency, the failure to engage enough stakeholders in the process, and discounting the role of inertia. Old habits and attitudes of contentment and complacency frequently derail change.

For example, the leadership of a nonprofit company with which I am familiar speaks regularly of equity, inclusion, and diversity as central to its identity. Change efforts in this area have come in fits and starts and often fall short. Workgroups dedicated to equity and inclusion met regularly and passionately and made detailed recommendations to the larger company. Still, change toward greater equity, inclusion, and diversity was incomplete. Old habits and complacency inhibited innovation.

In *Leading Change,* John P. Kotter, Professor of Leadership, Emeritus, at Harvard Business School, outlines an eight-step process for leading and managing change. His insights have become the foundation for leading change in organizations and businesses across six continents. In times such as ours, when change is upon us like a raft plummeting down whitewater rapids, Kotter's findings remain powerfully relevant.

Kotter asserts that seventy percent of change efforts in organizations fail due to the lack of a holistic approach. Whether you are a facilitator, executive coach, or leader of a company or nonprofit, Kotter's eight steps can help you navigate hard-charging waters with skill and finesse.

Step One: Create a Sense of Urgency

The objective in Step One is to create a visceral, gut-level drive to change that engages the whole company or organization. People need to leave their comfort zone and enter an area of anxiety where change is seen as not only necessary but essential. Survival is at stake.

Complacency often develops when things are going well, market share is stable, or reviews are positive. At such times, people bop along in systemic denial of the rapids ahead. Comfort is the enemy. Contentment kills. Satisfaction leads to stasis. Stasis leads to drowning in whitewater rapids.

In contrast, urgency is when all in the company are on the edge of their seats, paddles grasped firmly, eyes fixed on the goal ahead. Urgency is when everyone in your nonprofit or company sees both great dangers and opportunities every day. Urgency is not created by directives from on high or special reports. Urgency is created by leaders who aim for the heart and connect with the deepest aspirations of the entire organization.

Step Two: Creating the Guiding Coalition

The essence of Step Two is to assemble a group with enough clout to lead the change until it is woven into the warp and woof of the organization's fabric. This is no task for one person alone. Pardon the change in metaphors, but a single trumpet does not make a symphony. Groups of leaders, acting in harmony, are the only effective way to produce long-term, sustainable change. The task is to develop the right vision, communicate it to every soul in the organization, eliminate key obstacles, and generate short-term wins. Lone rangers cannot do these tasks.

The guiding coalition must have sufficient diversity and multiple points of view to generate the best ideas and strategies. It must have credibility across all levels and divisions of the organization for the change initiatives to be taken seriously by all employees. Recruit change leaders from the whole organization. Establish system-wide trust and crystal-clear objectives.

A team of leaders such as this needs time to bond and develop a full strategy. One-hour meetings spread over months will create neither urgency nor an empowered, guiding coalition. These goals are best met by holding retreats off-site for change leaders where creative magic can generate singleness of purpose, impassioned ownership, and the conviction that change is not only essential but inevitable for the company.

When putting together a Guiding Coalition, the team should have enough key players on board from all levels of the organization that those not included cannot block the change initiative. Including only managers, top executives, and board members will not get the job done.

Step Three: Developing a Change Vision

A change vision simplifies a multitude of other, more detailed decisions. This vision is aspirational and motivates people to take hard, painful, and courageous steps. Vision efficiently coordinates the actions of disparate people. A clear, compelling, motivating vision accomplishes what micro-management and authoritarian orders can never do.

In his *Second Inaugural Address* near the end of the Civil War, President Abraham Lincoln cast an aspirational vision.

> *"With malice toward none, with charity for all, with firmness in the right as God gives us to see the right, let us strive on to finish the work we are in, to bind up the nation's wounds, to care for him who shall have borne the battle and for his widow and his orphan, to do all which may achieve and cherish a just and lasting peace among ourselves and with all nations."*

Lincoln's vision brought a wounded nation to a higher purpose of charity, healing, and peace. His words have inspired millions and still move us to tears. More than one-hundred-fifty years since first spoken, they lift us up to our highest ideals and call forth action to be charitable, peace-loving, and repairers of the broken.

One-hundred years later, President John F. Kennedy's words conveyed urgency as well.

"I believe that this nation should commit itself to achieving the goal, before this decade is out, of landing a man on the moon and returning him safely to the Earth."

His compelling words demanded a collective response. These words were uttered on May 25, 1961, in the heat of the space race with the Soviet Union. Merely eight years later, on July 20, 1969, Astronaut Neil Armstrong took his first step on the moon. Urgency, combined with vision, made it happen.

Here are examples of change visions from the nonprofit and business worlds:

"We will feed every hungry child and house every hurting family until poverty is no more."

"To become the world's most loved, most flown, most profitable airline."

Vision flows through these statements. When owned by the whole organization, a compelling vision lifts the organization to real systemic change.

Step Four: Communicating the Vision for Buy-In

All employees, board members, and other stakeholders need to understand the change vision and be its ambassadors. In complex organizations, vision must be communicated through every means available: email, posters, meetings, presentations, business cards, and brochures. One directive in a memo by the CEO or Executive Director will not do it.

Change vision statements must be memorable. No excess words allowed and no babble. No jargon. Clean and simple truths trump wordy statements. Communicating a vision well requires practices that turn dull annual meetings into occasions for engagement.

Equally important is to walk the talk. Actions speak powerfully. If an organization says it believes in equity and inclusion, then meetings dominated by a few are out. Conduct must be consistent with words. Walking the talk sends a powerful message to everyone in the organization.

Step Five: Enabling Broad-Based Action

The internal structures of companies often block them from living the vision. An organization that says its vision is to strengthen customer service might have senior managers who second-guess new, innovative ways of listening to customers' needs. Lower managers closest to the delivery of services are dismissed as having less knowledge than so-called experts at the top of the food chain. Instead, they should be invited to bring forward their best ideas. The biggest impediment to living the vision is senior managers who feel threatened by loss of control. Engaging all employees in the change vision is always best.

Step Six: Generating Short-Term Wins

Celebrate successes as soon as possible. Changing the culture of an organization or its service delivery model usually takes a long time—years, not months. Therefore, celebrating small victories and communicating those victories to the whole organization is essential. The achievements must be related to the vision for change. Small successes generate momentum and communicate to cynics and naysayers that the change vision is charging ahead.

Step Seven: Don't Let Up!

Stick with the program relentlessly until the new equilibrium takes over. Voices that resisted the change will grow quiet for a while, maybe even cheer it. Then they will suggest a pause to consolidate the progress. That pause will cause a systemic change to lose momentum. Instead, keep engaging more people and adding more projects. Keep lifting the change vision in all communication forms. Keep building a sense of urgency and provide proof that the change initiative is working. Finally, recognize that changing an organization's entire approach or culture takes a long time to achieve. Do not declare victory too soon. Instead, stay the course.

Step Eight: Make It Stick

Changing the culture of an organization involves vision and living core values every day. Changing the entire organization requires changing organizational practices over a long period. Tradition and inertia are powerful forces that resist change. Old habits die hard, and new habits take repeated practice. Success must be visible. Those who refuse to get on board must go. (Sorry, folks.) Bring new employees on board with enthusiasm and a commitment that they, too, are essential to the organization's transformation. The values and practices must be fully embedded for the change to stick. Only when change is adopted by the majority of employees and other stakeholders will success be sustained long term.

Systemic change is difficult. If you expect to lead a system-wide change effort, I recommend you use John Kotter's full program. Create urgency, gather a winning coalition with a critical mass, build and communicate vision, empower broad-based action, celebrate short-term wins, and make it stick. Thrive!

Coming to Terms with Organizational History

Coming to terms with an organization's history through the Timeline Exercise is a great way for an organization to discover new energy, heal wounds, or come to terms with unhealthy behaviors. The exercise helps a group see patterns of internal and external conduct as if in a rear view mirror. By recognizing these patterns, a group can choose new, healthier behaviors. The exercise takes about two hours and inspires groups with the results.

The timeline reconstructs a portion of an organization's history. It examines how the economy, political events, and local factors shaped the organization during that time. Groups also look at their activities, decisions, leadership changes, and new initiatives in the same period. They look at times of lethargy and decline, and moments of strength and innovation. Insights emerge with mindfulness of environmental circumstances and internal performance. Groups bond, get excited and discover they can reinvent best moments. They imagine a healthier, more robust future. When combined with other planning methods, such as strategic planning, the Timeline Exercise helps an organization develop a road map for ongoing success.

How It Works

No matter what size group you are working with, conduct the Timeline Exercise in a room with a long wall. Before the meeting, attach a long sheet of butcher paper to the wall. If you need to, run the paper along one wall and around the corner onto a second wall.

In a bold color across the top, write five-year intervals, such as 1990, 1995, 2000, 2005, 2010, 2015, with big spaces between years. In a column on the paper's far left edge, list the following, with lots of room between each heading: Nation and World, Economy, Neighborhood, and [the organization's name].

	1990	1995	2000	2005	2010	2015
Nation & World						
Economy						
Neighborhood						
Our Organization						

Seat participants in a semi-circle in front of the wall and give a marker to each person. After you give directions, invite everyone to come forward to write information on the butcher paper. Cross talk at the wall is part of the fun of this exercise and builds energy for the rest of the event. If the group is too large for everyone to come forward, invite them to remain seated while they call out items for a scribe to write on the timeline.

Have the group begin by writing key national and international events on the wall under the appropriate years. Groups typically list wars, cultural events, and changes in the American presidency. Next, invite them to record economic developments in the various time frames: recessions, recoveries, real estate upturns and declines, periods of new construction, periods of boom and bust. Third, have the group list local or neighborhood events. These might include changes in city leadership, racial unrest, new planning initiatives, and businesses opening or closing. Local dramatic events get listed here, too, such as shootings, plant closures, and new highways that eliminated a neighborhood or cut a community in half.

Recording these events helps the group see the external context in which they have operated.

The most important part of the timeline exercise occurs when groups record their organizational history. Stories emerge of when the group was first organized, who was involved, and the excitement that fueled their beginning. Leadership changes are noted and major decisions listed. People record when new ventures and programs were launched and when decline set in. Moments of discovery happen as the group sees key internal events in the broader context of what was happening locally, nationally, and globally.

The facilitator asks the group, "What do you notice?" "What do you wonder?" and waits for participants to share. Insights pour forth. When sharing stalls, the facilitator asks, "What else do you notice?" "What is emerging for you now?" "Who hasn't shared his or her insights?"

Asking such questions leads to ah-ha moments. Eureka! The group discovers patterns in their behavior. They see how the broader context contributed to vibrancy, decline, or stasis.

I was working in Troy, New York, an old industrial city in the Capital District of New York in the 1990s. During that time, the city declared bankruptcy and the State of New York imposed a financial control board on the city council. The town was a mess. Abandoned housing pitted the landscape. Businesses were empty shells. Once a bustling industrial center that supplied horseshoes, pot-bellied stoves, and men's shirt collars for a growing nation, Troy had lost twenty-seven percent of its population since the 1950s. If a city can be clinically depressed, Troy was.

A few local leaders decided to see if we could turn the city around. With chutzpah and hope, we crawled back from disaster. A banker, an executive director of an affordable housing agency, the president of the local Chamber of Commerce, the director of a mental health agency, an architect, a couple of planners, an accountant, a former city manager, and I met regularly. I was both pastor of a Presbyterian church in downtown Troy and president of the affordable housing agency. My background in community organizing came in handy.

We founded the Troy Civic Partnership. During our second meeting, I led the group in a Timeline Exercise. Meeting in the fellowship hall of the Presbyterian church, we spread a long sheet of butcher paper on one wall. We marked five-year intervals from 1930 to the present. I asked the group to record on the chart what was happening in the national and international context. They listed the Great Depression, World War II, the post-war boom, and recessions that popped up periodically.

Next, I invited them to list what was happening in the community. They mentioned the industrial renaissance during World War II, the population that grew after the War, and the closing of the shirt factories in the 1960s. They described the decline of the city in the late sixties. They lamented the tearing down of city blocks in the name of urban renewal during the 1970s. They reminisced about historic architecture lost forever. They listed the downtown mall—a venture that flopped big time. They mentioned the closing of schools and the fleeing of populations to the suburbs. It was grim. However, we were talking.

I asked the group to tell the city's founding story—its creation story. What I got back was a rush of enthusiasm about the first water-powered factory in upstate New York that fueled the industrial revolution in America. They celebrated Rensselaer Polytechnic University, their highly-ranked engineering school, and Russell Sage College for Women; and all the innovation that emerged from their scholars and students over the decades. They recalled the men's removable shirt collar invented in Troy. It permitted men to have clean collars multiple times each day without needing to change their shirts. In its heyday, Troy had more shirt collar factories than any other place in America. They mentioned multiple instances of corruption by local party bosses. They celebrated the preservation movement that had protected much of the city's stunning 19th Century architecture. All these moments in history were on the timeline chart. Wow.

I invited the group to make observations, asking, "What do you notice?" "What do you wonder?" The group responded,

> "We were inventors."
>
> "We were entrepreneurs."
>
> "We innovated."
>
> "We took risks and embraced a changing world with new technology."
>
> "We haven't done that in a long time."
>
> "We used to have people who were smart engineers and investors."

I asked the group, "What does your timeline tell you that we need to do?" The group responded, "Be innovative, experiment, invest in new ventures."

Months later, with leadership from our group, Troy became the home of the Capital District Regional Arts Center. Located along the waterfront of the Hudson River in a row of empty townhouses built in the 1860s, the Art Center became a magnet for economic growth. Soon after the Art

Center launched, a bagel shop opened next door. A victory! Artists rented lofts and opened studios. More businesses opened and the streets of Troy began to fill with people. Slowly, the City of Troy turned around. We celebrated every new business. The Troy Civic Partnership and its leaders were credited with the city's transformation from bankruptcy to economic stability. It all began with a handful of leaders who cared and a Timeline Exercise.

Context profoundly shapes the way organizations make decisions. Becoming more mindful of context, combined with awareness about the patterns of behavior in a group is the purpose of the Timeline Exercise. The strengths of the past can form the foundation of the future. The problems of the past need not be repeated. With self-awareness, groups can change the future. They can choose to write new chapters, reinvent themselves, and thrive.

Recording Meeting Results

Recording meeting results accurately and succinctly is an important task for effective meetings. Detailing decisions reached, documenting action items, and listing key ideas keeps an organization on track. Well-written minutes minimize confusion and increase clarity. Recording meetings may take many forms: minutes, notes, verbatim transcripts, video, and audio recording, and one of the most innovative—graphic recording.

Minutes may include the following:

- The meeting date

- The time the meeting started

- The meeting location

- Names of participants

- Review and correction of previous minutes

- Agenda review and additional items

- Actions taken

- Next steps

- Items that will be held over for the next meeting

- Next meeting date, time, and location

- Time of adjournment

Note that minutes need not record everything. Avoid recording the details of discussions, volatile comments, and personal opinions. Edit minutes carefully and delete unnecessary words. The simpler, the better. Full sentences may not be required. Clearly written action items are essential.

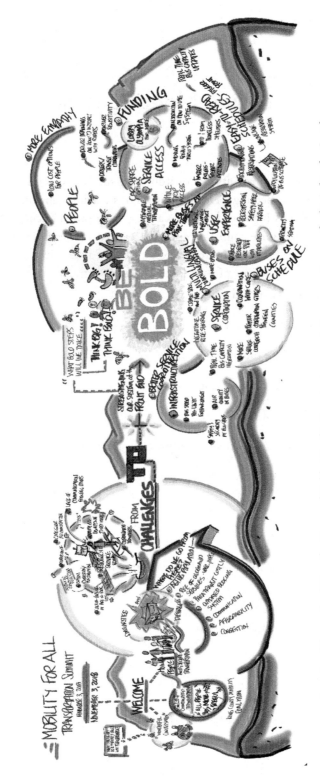

Sample of the work of Timothy Corey of Colibri Facilitation at a transportation summit we co-facilitated in the Seattle area.

An alternative to recording minutes during meetings is audio/video recording. Every smart device has a microphone and a camera available to record meetings accurately. Seek the permission of the group to record the proceedings. Precision is guaranteed when drafting minutes after the meeting.

Graphic recording is growing in popularity as a visual way to record meetings. Graphic recording is particularly helpful for people who process information visually (visual learners), as well as those who are deaf or hearing impaired. Even people like me, who primarily learn through words, feelings, and intuition; appreciate the power of images to convey meaning.

Graphic recording, graphic facilitation, and mind-mapping are similar methods to capture a group's conversations in images and phrases. A graphic recorder distills the essence of the meeting with images, pictures, words, and color in real time. On the previous page is a sample of the work of Timothy Corey of Colibri Facilitation at a transportation summit we co-facilitated in the Seattle area.

This graphic recording documents the entire six-hour meeting in one comprehensive image. Even participants who are not visual learners can quickly grasp the essence of the summit's discussions.

When graphic recording combines with traditional meeting facilitation, more participants feel included. Those who are not adept at speaking in public feel understood when they see the meaning of their words displayed. This increases participation and fosters trust.

Graphic recordings weave insights and diverse perspectives into a tapestry of meaning. The composite picture reflects the collective imagination of everyone who has participated. The display helps participants remember their joint efforts and can be shared with others to frame what occurred in the conference or event.

The following graphic recording summarizes the method and beauty of graphic recording.

Graphic recording is a growing practice, with workshops offered online. Graphic recorders typically charge similar rates to professional facilitators. They can be a great, energizing addition to your meeting, conference, or summit.

Explanation of a Graphic Recording, by Jessamy Gee, Think in Colour

The Art of Wrapping Up

As meetings near their end, three steps remain: 1) summarize the actions, 2) evaluate what went well and what to strengthen, and 3) closing remarks.

Summarizing, evaluating, and closing remarks accomplish the following:

- Clarity about outcomes, next steps, and the person or group responsible for implementation.

- Agreement about what was discussed and decided.

- Clarity about what went well and what did not.

- Engaged participants who know their voices matter.

- Evaluations that help planners design better meetings.

- Final remarks that anchor a positive spirit and a job well done.

Summarizing can take many forms. Choosing a method depends on the size of the meeting, how the event is structured, and the available time. The most common practice that works for groups of all sizes is to have the facilitator tick through a list of action items out loud. Simultaneously writing each actionable outcome on a flip chart, whiteboard, or electronic display makes them visible. Saying the key points out loud in a concise manner helps the whole group anchor the outcomes in their memories and reinforces commitment to next steps.

If you have a larger meeting or conference that employed a graphic recorder, have him or her display and speak about the final graphic drawing. This approach helps both auditory and visual learners to hear and see the meeting's outcomes. For persons with sight or hearing impairment, utilizing the gifts of the graphic recorder who both speaks and draws can be a powerful way to wrap up a meeting.

Another way to summarize meeting results in groups of thirty or less is the "popcorn" style report. The facilitator invites the group randomly to say out loud one key actionable item. Allow the group members to "pop-out" each item until all the key actions are named. Record each item visually on whatever media you have available: flip charts, electronic screens, whiteboards, blackboards, whatever works. A skilled facilitator will encourage the group by asking questions like, "What have we missed?" "What have we left out?" "Does anyone who hasn't spoken recall an action item we missed in our summary?"

If you have more time to summarize a meeting, particularly with a summit, multi-day conference or a retreat, take fifteen minutes and hold a *1-2-4-All* exercise more fully described in the chapter, *The Art of Liberating Structures*. Invite each person for one minute to write down key decisions or accomplishments on a sheet of paper. Next, invite them to form pairs. For two minutes share thoughts and key actions. Then ask them to create groups of four. For four more minutes share key ideas and action steps. Encourage them to notice similar themes, insights, and converging thoughts. Have each quad write down the key thoughts. Writing them down encourages discipline and draws from another part of the brain. The combination of speaking and writing engenders clarity and focus. Then, in the whole group, invite each group of four to announce out loud one key actionable step—one to a table or group of four. Make provision for recording each item. The whole *1-2-4-All* process is quick and amazingly democratic. No more than fifteen minutes is needed. All voices engage in summarizing outcomes, not only the facilitator and the verbally dominant.

Make sure the meeting notes or minutes record the outcomes in a clear, bulleted fashion. Highlight them at the top of the report. Surround them in a simple box and use arrows to emphasize the actions. Be sure to write each item with a short, active verb such as engage, recruit, research, write, build, and prepare. Keep each action item short and to the point.

The final step in any well-run meeting, other than going out for drinks and dinner, is the evaluation. When well-designed and used in every session, evaluations build better, more effective meetings and more productive organizations. Think of evaluations as the cheer at the end of a hard-fought game of soccer or basketball. It's always good to end with a cheer from the crowd and a team meeting with the coach to discuss what went well in the game and what did not.

Evaluations should address a handful of questions:

- What went well?

- What could have been better?

- Was the agenda clear?

- Did the meeting design engage all voices?

- Did the room set-up work? Could you hear and see all the materials and presentations?

- Were outcomes clear and well summarized?

- What feature, element, or agenda item did you like the most?

- What suggestions do you have for a better meeting next time?

Notice what I did not include. I did not ask participants to rank speakers on a scale of 1 to 5. I did not invite rankings on space, food, and drinks. Rankings mean next to nothing because they do not give meeting planners and facilitators specific ideas to strengthen the next round. When I see a poorly written evaluation, I toss it or use it to line the chicken coop. If I rank the food and refreshments as a three instead of a five, does that mean the coffee was average, the cookies stale, or the grapes discolored? The question and responses tell meeting planners nothing about next steps. Ask questions that evoke meaningful responses.

If you do use a grading or ranking system because you cannot break the habit, ask a follow-up question such as, "Why did you grade the item as you did?" Asking this kind of question results in tidbits of wisdom that will make your next meeting go better.

Finally, end with a word of encouragement. When meetings get long, and participants are eager to get to their next meeting, go fishing, or flee to Hawaii, we are tempted to end abruptly. In short meetings, it is usually sufficient for the facilitator to say something brief such as "Thank you for coming. Good job. See you next week." However, if you are coming to the end of a retreat, an annual conference, or a dicey, all-day meeting on tough issues, it is better if you dedicate time to ending the event with a few open-ended, creative questions:

- What did you notice about our meeting today and what do you wonder about that would help next time we meet?

- What surprised you?

- What ways did you learn, grow, or hear new insights?

- What gives you hope?

Encourage people to write down their responses silently for one minute and then invite a few to share. The reason leaders ask such questions is that all of us need stories of hope, perseverance, and growth. Even the most cynical come to meetings with a glimmer of hope that the meeting or conference will make a difference.

People from all cultures and backgrounds aspire to make meetings worth their time. Inviting conferees to name successes, insights, and discoveries lifts them to their best. Gratitude and courage always trump boredom and disengagement. End meetings with affirmation and your meetings, even the most difficult ones, will result in more people believing meetings can work and work well.

When ending meetings that are long, emotionally demanding or have stretched the participants in new directions, end with something affirming. Celebrate success. Affirm the gifts and contributions of everyone. Affirm even the guy in love with his voice. Affirm everyone, and your meetings will end with hope and a glimmer of light.

The Art of Writing Well

Facilitators need to be good writers. We write emails, proposals, letters, reports, and articles. Our clients expect clarity, not gobbledygook. Unfortunately, many professionals write bloated, jargon-filled bilge. Long, complicated sentences with lots of three- and four-syllable words may seem impressive, even knowledgeable, but are not helpful. Writing that is easy to understand makes clients happy.

Books on business writing and nonfiction writing with tips on writing well are easy to find. My favorites are *On Writing Well* by William Zinsser and *5000 Words per Hour: Write Faster, Write Smarter* by Chris Fox.

Good writing is hard work. When you have a writing project, protect your writing time fiercely. Eliminate disruptions. Turn off your Internet, emails, and alerts. Mute your phone and turn it upside down away from you or put it in a different room. Tell your family or coworkers that this time is for one purpose: writing. Grab a favorite refreshment and close your door. Write. If you stop breathing, you have permission to call 911. Do not stop writing.

Let it flow. Even if you don't know how to begin your document, start writing. You need to get the juices running. Do not stop to edit, especially when writing longer documents. Don't correct typos. Do not rework and rework. Just write. Writing comes more easily once you're in the flow of writing, so you don't want to break the flow. Editing comes later and engages another portion of the brain.

As you write, use short words, short sentences, and short paragraphs. Most people can follow only one thought at a time. If you string along multiple ideas in one sentence, people will get lost in a tangle of phrases. Pare the verbiage. As a facilitator, consultant, or leader, you want your writing to be easily understood.

Use active verbs. Depending on how you word a sentence, a verb can be either **active** or **passive**. When you use the active voice, the subject of the sentence does the action:

> The meeting *halted.*

> The facilitator *stopped* the meeting.

When you use the passive voice, the action is done to the subject.

> The meeting *was halted.*

> The meeting *was stopped* by the facilitator.

Active voice has strength and energy. You feel the energy when you read, "The facilitator stopped the meeting." Compare that to the passivity of "The meeting was stopped by the facilitator." Use active verbs.

Notice the change in these examples:

> When the consideration of all factors was taken into account, the implementation process proceeded.

> The process continued once the group considered all factors.

> The mission and purpose of the Do Good Association are to create a sustainable, inclusive, and democratic society by including all voices and advocating for workable solutions for our communities that are underserved and demand justice.

> The Do Good Association builds just and equitable democratic communities. We welcome all voices. We work with underserved communities that demand justice.

Short, punchy words and sentences trump long words and long sentences. You are not aspiring to write like the United States Department of Defense with its defensive capability, and technological, organizational, and administrative competencies. Your role models write short and sweet: Lincoln, Thoreau, Hemingway, and the like.

"Four score and seven years ago …" (Abraham Lincoln, *The Gettysburg Address*).

"I went to the woods because I wished to live deliberately, to front only the essential facts of life, and see if I could not learn what it had to teach, and not, when I came to die, discover that I had not lived" (Henry David Thoreau, *Walden*).

"He was an old man who fished alone in a skiff in the Gulf Stream and he had gone eighty-four days now without taking a fish" (Ernest Hemingway, *The Old Man and the Sea*).

See how elegant, how simple, how direct? No jargon. No long words. No stacked-up stacks of bureaucratic, bombastic, and boring bilge.

Words such as write, act, explore, complete, bridge, jump, and build bring action to writing. Unnecessarily long words such as implementation, transformation, and sustainability weigh the reader down. Instead of transformation use "change." When tempted to use a three- or four-syllable word, choose a word with one or two syllables. Your writing will have more life and energy. Your reader will stay awake.

When it is time to edit, be merciless. Chop, slash, and burn. Rid all excess. Shorten sentences. Shorten paragraphs. Eliminate adverbs. Reduce adjectives to a minimum. Let your nouns be naked, devoid of clothing. I know that your seventh-grade English teacher, like mine, may have told you to adorn your creative writing with lush, flowery adjectives, and rich, vivid adverbs:

Bounding excitedly through long fields of bright, yellow daffodils and tip-toeing through vast expanses of vivid red tulips with the ease of a graceful teenage kangaroo being chased by a rabid, brown-spotted dingo, Gertrude fondly remembered her fun-packed morning had begun auspiciously with the birth of four adorable pups who resembled the now foaming canine.

Mrs. Grimace might have been happy with those adjectives. Your client will not be. Complexity confuses. Simple trumps foaming, flowery fulminations.

Chop. Fold. Mutilate. Eliminate those awful noun clusters that sound like the National Association of Sustainability and Implementation Procedures Administration wrote them. Stringing together noun clusters does not make you sound important. It makes you seem confused.

Edit *everything* you write: articles, news items, proposals, and emails, too. Editing takes time and work. Do it anyway. If you can stomach it, read your text backward. Your brain will be less likely to skip over typos and misspellings. Your readers will thank you for your effort. Let clarity, brevity, and simplicity abound!

Assembling a Facilitator's Toolkit

You never know when you will need resources to make a meeting run well. I carry in my car a well-stocked, traveling toolkit for facilitating meetings on the spot. My Boy Scout leader taught me to "be prepared," and prepared I am.

I cannot count the times I attend a meeting and discover the planners forgot to bring materials for recording results. I dig into my briefcase. Out come artist tape (better for walls than masking tape); brightly colored non-toxic, unscented markers; and my personal favorite—giant post-it notes.

My briefcase is heavy. Besides worn copies of Tolstoy's *War and Peace* and *Ulysses* by James Joyce, I carry a laser pointer, a spare thumb drive, and a corkscrew. Hey, I never know when I'll be called upon to facilitate a meeting or open a bottle of wine. Optional for the briefcase: a bottle of wine.

In my car, I keep large flip chart paper (24" x 36"), a collapsible tripod, flower vases with artificial flowers, and a handful of brightly colored table cloths. I have a large screen projector, extension cords, and mini-speakers in my office closet. I'm ready to go for the next facilitation gig. Assemble your own facilitator's toolkit for your events. Be prepared!

Here's a checklist of what you might need for your events. Some items will come from your stash. The hosting organizations will provide some. Some may need to be rented for the occasion.

- Digital camera—for recording meeting results and photographing happy people. The photos (with permission) can be used to illustrate reports, enliven your website, and market future events.

- Laptop fully charged and charger cable.

- Sound system. I travel with a small speaker system. Today's technology is amazing. Tiny speakers and a little amp hooked up to a laptop can belt it out. Very cool.

- Large screen projector. Do not skimp on foot candles. Bright is beautiful.

- Microphone system. While usually provided by the hosting organization, take your own. Test the one provided for you before the meeting begins. Test all the electronic paraphernalia. Make sure they work. If they don't work well, use your own.

- Extension cord and power strip.

- Screen or blank wall. If live captioning is provided, you will need two large screens.

- Round café tables 36" to 48" across. Four tables will seat up to twenty people. An alternative is to rent tables. In a pinch, you can use eight-foot tables with two people on each side and no one on the ends. You want conversation and intimacy.

- Tables for refreshments and registration. Rectangular tables work fine.

- Chairs.

- Red and white checkered tablecloths, plastic or cloth. Other colors and patterns are fine, too.

- Colorful table runners from different cultures.

- Stuffed animals. Whether we are two-years-old or ninety-two, stuffed animals help when tensions mount.

- Name tags. Preprinted names work well if done in a large font. Otherwise, use blank nametags and encourage participants to write big!

- Flip chart paper, usually 24" x 36". I prefer the style with an adhesive strip.

- Tripod to hold the flip chart paper.

- White artist tape. Do not use masking or painter's tape. They damage walls.

- Rolling whiteboards or a roll of butcher paper and a long wall or multiple flip chart tripods.

- Giant post-it notes for collecting and posting key ideas. I love the 11" x 11" size. My second choice is 8" x 6". Smaller sizes cannot be read by eyes with sight impairment. Big and bold beat puny and paltry. Teach people to write big!

- Notecards of different sizes for place cards, memory joggers, and various exercises.

- 8.5" x 11" lined paper for registering attendance and taking notes.

- Pencils and pens.

- Stapler, staples, and staple remover.

- Rubber bands.

- Screwdrivers, a small box of screws, scissors, pliers, small hammer, and vise grips. Seriously.

- Duct tape. A facilitator's best buddy. Use it for taping extension, microphone, and computer cords to the floor and fixing everything except dinner.

- Non-toxic, unscented, colorful, broad-tipped markers. Blue, green, dark brown, red, orange, and black can be seen. Avoid light colors.

- Mugs or cups to hold markers.

- Plastic vases with plastic flowers. Lots of them. We're aiming for festive.

- Non-toxic, unscented votive candles. Candles with batteries and a tiny light work well.

- First Aid kit.

- Facial tissues.

- A bell or chime to call time. I prefer a chime. Tibetan finger cymbals are also cool.

- Refreshments. Set a table with a combination of healthy and unhealthy choices: fruit, veggies, finger food, chips, and what not. Include favorite beverages. Design the setup for persons with mobility disabilities. Oh yes, chocolate!

- Water. Lots of it.

- Cash for tipping. You will need tips to say, "Thank you," to custodians, chefs, wait staff, and parking attendants. Be generous.

- Business cards.

- A donkey. Carrying all this stuff can be taxing. A large suitcase with wheels also works well.

Ten Reasons to Hire a Professional Facilitator

The goal of this book is to introduce you, the reader, to a host of meeting facilitation tools and techniques. Whether you have been facilitating meetings for decades or have attended only a few meetings, I hope that you will be better equipped to design and lead inclusive meetings with skill and finesse. Whether you are facilitating a weekly staff meeting, a workgroup, or a board meeting, I am confident that you will find in THRIVE insights and encouragement to facilitate meetings of all kinds.

Nevertheless, there are times when hiring a professional facilitator is the right choice (Hiring me helps pay my mortgage). Facilitating a retreat, strategic plan, or conflicted group takes skill, energy, time, and experience. Many organizations have the skills internally to facilitate a retreat or strategic plan, and some do not. Here are ten reasons why hiring a professional facilitator may be the right choice for your organization.

1. Professional facilitators are avid readers in the art of strategic thinking, expert facilitation, and whole systems change. They bring a best-practices mindset to their work.

2. A professional facilitator has worked with dozens of groups and is equipped to respond to nearly every setting imaginable.

3. A professional facilitator asks dozens of questions. Creative questions allow a composite picture of the organization to emerge before a strategy event. This listening prepares the consultant to facilitate with knowledge and skill.

4. A professional facilitator designs a planning process that is unique to you. Every group is different. Missions vary, and people are different. The strategic challenges differ. An experienced facilitator creates meeting designs with you from a reservoir of applications.

5. Events facilitated by a professional engage the imagination, generate energy, and build ownership across the organization. They are less likely to be boring, frustrating, or wasteful.

6. A professional facilitator is neutral, bringing objectivity and focusing on the best process. An external facilitator sees and hears what an insider cannot.

7. A skilled facilitator can manage conflict with poise and remain objective. Conflict becomes a creative tool rather than something about which to be anxious.

8. A professional facilitator will help your group get specific about action plans. She or he will not let you get stuck with vague generalities.

9. Professional facilitators bring a love of people and facilitating groups. They bring joy, humor, and seasoning to your group.

10. A professional facilitator brings the intangible: a spirit that draws people together, an emotional maturity that helps the group remain focused, and an enthusiasm that helps the group stay engaged.

Conclusion

I hope this book has been helpful. It is an accumulation of decades of research, reading, and practice. I learned long ago that the praxis model of learning makes a lot of sense—combining theory and practice makes for great learning. This is doubly true for meeting facilitators. Read the book, then get out and lead meetings. Open the relevant chapter and try a few ideas. Then re-read it and try again. After four decades of being a leader and facilitator, I am still hungry for new steps, new insights, new learnings, and new ways to make meetings thrive.

Take baby steps, then walk, then run. If you are like any of my young granddaughters, once you've taken a few steps, you'll soon be sprinting. A whole new world of great, inclusive meetings will unfold before you.

Look beyond the horizon. See a beautiful land where people are centered, energized, and focused. See a beautiful tapestry of people—different yet welcomed, diverse and included. All have courage and voice. See a vision of meetings with great results, clarity of purpose, and passion-filled engagement. No boredom. No yawns. Only joyous, eager faces of every shade and perspective.

May your gifts and leadership flourish! May all your meetings be grounded in radical equality and a generous embrace of all! May all your meetings thrive!

Further Reading

Akdeniz, Can. *Key Questions in Strategic Planning.* San Bernardino, CA: First Publishing, 2015.

Allison, Michael and Jude Kaye. *Strategic Planning for Nonprofit Organizations: A Practical Guide for Dynamic Times.* (3rd Ed.) Hoboken, New Jersey: John Wiley and Sons, Inc., 2015.

Bell, Jeanne., Jan Masaoka and Steve Zimmerman. *Nonprofit Sustainability: Making Strategic Decisions for Financial Viability.* San Francisco: Berrett-Koehler Publishers, Inc., 2010.

Block, Peter. *Flawless Consulting: A Guide to Getting Your Expertise Used.* (3rd Ed.) San Francisco: Jossey-Bass, 2001.

Brown, Jennifer. *Inclusion: Diversity, The New Workplace and The Will to Change.* (2nd Ed.) Hartford, CT: Publish Your Purpose Press, 2016.

Brown, Juanita and David Isaacs. *The World Café: Shaping Our Futures Through Conversations That Matter.* San Francisco: Berrett-Koehler Publishers, Inc., 2005.

Brown, Juanita and Thomas J. Hurley. *"Conversational Leadership: Thinking Together for a Change."* The Systems Thinker. Vol. 20, No. 9, Nov. 2009.

Brown, Michael Jacoby. *Building Powerful Community Organizations: A Personal Guide to Creating Groups that Can Solve Problems and Change the World.* Arlington, MA: Long Haul Press, 2006.

Bryce, Herrington. *Financial and Strategic Management for Nonprofit Organizations.* (2nd Ed.) Englewood Cliffs, NJ: Prentice Hall, 1992.

Bunker, Barbara Benedict and Billie T. Alban. *Large Group Interventions: Engaging the Whole System for Rapid Change.* San Francisco: Jossey-Bass Publishers, 1997.

Café to Go! A Quick Reference Guide for Hosting World Café. The World Café Community Foundation. WWW.THEWORLDCAFE.COM. 2015.

Cashman, Kevin. *The Pause Principle: Step Back to Lead Forward.* San Francisco: Berrett-Koehler Publishers, Inc., 2012.

Chait, Richard P., William P. Ryan and Barbara E. Taylor. *Governance as Leadership: Reframing the Work of Nonprofit Boards.* Hoboken, New Jersey: John Wiley and Sons, Inc., 2005.

Cohen, Dan S. *The Heart of Change Field Guide: Tools and Tactics for Leading Change in Your Organization.* Boston: Harvard Business School Press, 2005.

Cooperrider, David., Diana Whitney and Jacqueline M. Stavros. *Appreciative Inquiry Handbook: For Leaders of Change.* (2nd Ed.) San Francisco: Berrett-Koehler Publishers, Inc., 2008.

Corder, Honorée. *You Must Write a Book: Boost Your Brand, Get More Business, and Become the Go-To Expert.* (2nd Ed.) Honorée Enterprises Publishing, 2018.

Fisher, Roger and William Ury. *Getting to Yes: Negotiating Agreement Without Giving In.* (2nd Ed.) New York: Penguin Books, 1991.

Freire, Paulo. *Pedagogy of the Oppressed.* (Trans. Bergman Ramos, Myra). New York: The Seabury Press, 1973.

Grace, Kay Sprinkel, Amy McClellan and John A. Yankey. *The Nonprofit Board's Role in Mission, Planning, and Evaluation.* (2nd Ed.) Washington D.C.: BoardSource, 2009.

Hammond, Sue Annis. *The Thin Book of Appreciative Inquiry.* (2nd Ed.) Bend, OR: Thin Book Publishing Co., 1998.

Harder, Cameron. *Discovering the Other: Asset-Based Approaches for Building Community Together.* Herndon, VA: Alban Institute, 2013.

Heietz, Ronald, Alexander Grashow and Marty LInsky. *The Practice of Adaptive Leadership: Tools and Tactics for Changing Your Organization and the World.* Boston: Harvard Business Press, 2009.

Hennessey, Ray, Editor. *Write Your Business Plan.* Entrepreneur Press, 2015.

Hollins, Caprice and Isla Govan. *Diversity, Equity, and Inclusion: Strategies for Facilitating Conversations on Race.* Lanham, MD: Rowman and Littlefield, 2015.

Hurley, Thomas J. and Juanita Brown. *Conversational Leadership: Thinking Together for a Change.* Systems Thinker. Pegasus Communications, Inc., 2009.

Jacobs, Robert W. *Real Time Strategic Change: How to Involve an Entire Organization in Fast and Far-Reaching Change.* San Francisco: Berrett-Koehler Publishers, Inc., 1997.

Johnson, Sarai. *Strategic Planning That Actually Works: A Step-by-Step Guide to Get it Done Faster, Cheaper, and Better Than Ever.* Eugene, OR: Teknia Publishing, 2015.

Kaner, Sam. *Facilitator's Guide to Participatory Decision-making.* (3rd Ed.) San Francisco: Jossey-Bass, 2014.

Katcher, Bruce L. *An Insider's Guide to Building a Successful Consulting Practice.* New York: Amacon, 2010.

Kotter, John P. *Leading Change.* Boston: Harvard Business Review Press, 2012.

Lafley, A.G. and Roger L. Martin. *Playing to Win: How Strategy Really Works.* Boston: Harvard Business Review Press. 2013.

LaForce, Tom. *Meeting Hero: Plan and Lead Productive Meetings.* Tom Laforce Self Published, 2014.

La Piana, David. *The Nonprofit Strategy Revolution: Real-Time Strategic Planning in a Rapid-Response World.* New York: Turner Publishing Company, 2008.

La Piana, David, Heather Gowdy, Lester Olmstead-Rose and Brent Copen. *The Nonprofit Business Plan: The Leader's Guide to Creating a Successful Business Model.* New York: Turner Publishing Company, 2012.

Law, H.F. Eric. *The Bush Was Blazing But Not Consumed.* St Louis: Chalice Press, 1996.

Law, H.F. Eric. *The Wolf Shall Dwell with the Lamb: A Spirituality for Leadership in a Multicultural Community.* St. Louis: Chalice Press, 1993.

Lipmanowicz, Henri and Keith McCandless. *The Surprising Power of Liberating Structures: Simple Rules to Unleash A Culture of Innovation.* Seattle: Liberating Structures Press, 2013.

Margulies, Nancy. *Mapping Inner Space: Learning and Teaching Visual Mapping.* (2nd Ed.) Tuscon, AZ: Zephyr Press, 2002.

McClean, David R. *Strategic Planning: Simple as A, B, C.* Morrisville, NC: Lulu Publishing Services, 2015.

Nadler, Reldan S. *Leading with Emotional Intelligence: Hands on Strategies for Building Confident and Collaborative Star Performers.* New York: McGraw Hill, 2011.

Neal, Craig and Patricia. *The Art of Convening: Authentic Engagement in Meetings, Gatherings and Conversations.* San Francisco: Berrett-Koehler Publishers, Inc., 2011.

O'Conner, Patricia T. *Woe Is I: The Grammarphobe's Guide to Better English in Plain English.* (3rd Ed.) New York: Riverhead Books, 2009.

Owen, Harrison. *Open Space Technology: A User's Guide.* (2nd Ed.) San Francisco: Berrett-Koehler Publishers, Inc., 1997.

Porter, Michael E. *On Strategy.* Boston: Harvard Business Review Press, 2011.

Rosengren, David B. *Building Motivational Interviewing Skills: A Practitioner Workbook.* New York: The Guilford Press, 2009.

Savage, John. *Listening and Caring Skills: A Guide for Groups and Leaders.* Nashville: Abington Press, 1996.

Schwarz, Roger. *Smart Leaders Smarter Teams: How You and Your Team Get Unstuck to Get Results.* San Francisco: Jossey-Bass, 2013.

Schwarz, Roger. *The Skilled Facilitator: A Comprehensive Resource for Consultants, Facilitators, Managers, Trainers, and Coaches.* San Francisco: Jossey-Bass, 2002.

Schwarz, Roger, Anne Davidson, Peg Carlson and Sue McKinney. *The Skilled Facilitator Fieldbook: Tips, Tools and Tested Methods for Consultants, Facilitators, Managers, Trainers, and Coaches.* San Francisco: Jossey-Bass, 2005.

Senge, Peter, Art Kleiner, Charlotte Roberts, Rick Ross and Bryan Smith. *The Fifth Discipline Fieldbook.* New York: Currency, 1994.

Seth, Christophe. *SWOT Analysis.* San Bernardino, CA: 50Minutes, 2015.

Sposato, Jonathan. *Better Together: Eight Way Working with Women Leads to Extraordinary Products and Profits.* Hoboken, New Jersey: John Wiley and Sons, Inc., 2018.

Steffens, Guillaume. *SMART Criteria: Become More Successful by Setting Better Goals.* San Bernardino, CA: 50Minutes, 2016.

Strunk, Jr., Strunk and E.B. White. *The Elements of Style.* (4th Ed.) New York: Penguin Books, 2000.

Taylor, Kathleen and Catherine Marienau. *Facilitating Learning with the Adult Brain in Mind: A Conceptual and Practical Guide.* San Francisco: Jossey-Bass, 2016.

Weisbord, Marvin and Sandra Janoff. *Future Search: An Action Guide to Finding Common Ground in Organizations and Communities.* (2nd Ed.) San Francisco: Berrett-Koehler Publishers, Inc., 2000.

Weiss, Alan. *Million Dollar Consulting Toolkit.* Hoboken, New Jersey: John Wiley and Sons, Inc., 2006.

Weiss, Alan. *Million Dollar Consulting Proposals: How to Write a Proposal That's Accepted Every Time.* Hoboken, New Jersey: John Wiley and Sons, Inc., 2012.

Wilson, Judith and Michelle Gislason. *Coaching Skills for Nonprofit Managers and Leaders: Developing People to Achieve Your Mission.* San Francisco: Jossey-Bass, 2010.

Zinsser, William. *On Writing Well: The Classic Guide to Writing Non-Fiction.* (7th Ed.) New York: HarperCollins Publishers, Inc., 2006.

INDEX

A Note from the Author

Thank you for reading *THRIVE: The Facilitator's Guide to Radically Inclusive Meetings*. I appreciate how valuable your time is, and I am delighted you chose to read my book. I hope it will be a resource that you will turn to again and again. If you have a spare moment, I would appreciate it if you would leave a review on the site where you purchased this book. Honest reviews help other readers find books they will enjoy and find valuable. If you'd like to send me an email, or find out when articles or blog posts are available, head to my website at *www.civicreinventions.com*.

Mark Smutny

HOW TO ENGAGE THE AUTHOR

BRING A SKILLED FACILITATOR, CONSULTANT,
SPEAKER AND AUTHOR TO
HELP YOUR ORGANIZATION THRIVE

— CONTACT —

CIVIC REINVENTIONS, INC.

1828 171st Place SE

Bothell, WA 98012

626-676-0287

mark.smutny@civicreinventions.com

Dr. MARK SMUTNY IS AVAILABLE FOR SPEAKING, CONSULTING,
FACILITATING CONFERENCES AND RETREATS,
COACHING AND TRAINING

— Building Inclusive Practices in Your Business or Nonprofit —

— Speaking, Keynotes, Presentations —

— Facilitating Annual Retreats, Summits, Conferences —

— Training in Listening Skills, Multicultural Facilitation, Inclusive Meeting Design —

— Executive Coaching —

Visit our website for more information on these services, free
resources and to sign up for our Blog.

www.civicreinventions.com